The Little Book
of
Kings and Queens
of Britain

The Little Book
of

Kings and Queens
of Britain

by

RODNEY CASTLEDEN

First published in 1999 by Mustard
Mustard is an imprint of Parragon

Parragon
Queen Street House
4 Queen Street
Bath BA1 1HE UK

Produced by Magpie Books, an imprint of
Robinson Publishing Ltd, London

Cover illustration courtesy of Superstock

ISBN 1 84164 264 9

A copy of the British Library Cataloguing-in-Publication Data is
available from the British Library

Contents

❦

Introduction

Britain has had kings and queens for over four thousand years. Most people know something of the monarchs who have reigned during the second millennium AD, starting with 1066 and the fateful Battle of Hastings. Before that our knowledge becomes patchy; everyone knows of Alfred, Arthur and Macbeth, few will have heard of Maelgwn and Carausius. But contemporary documents and king lists preserved in genealogies tell us that many more kings have ruled. The trail runs cold round about the time of Julius Caesar in the first century BC. Before that there are no documents, but the rich burials archaeologists have found show that there were kings in Britain two thousand years before Caesar, though we do not know their names.

For most of history, the key decisions have been made by monarchs. They have been the movers and shakers. Some have been powerful and effective, some inadequate, some obsessed with prestigious projects that did their subjects little good.

The glamour of monarchy has nevertheless always had its appeal. Many have been prepared to kill to become king – think of Macbeth and Richard III – and kingship has always been perilous. As Shakespeare's Richard II said,

"... within the hollow crown
That rounds the mortal temples of a king
Keeps Death his court."

1

❧

The Kings and Queens of Ancient Britain

Prehistoric Rulers

❧

In the neolithic (about 4500–2200 BC) people seem to have been roughly equal in status. Community decisions were possibly made by discussion, with a village bigman acting as chairman. People were buried with few grave goods, and none that show kingly power. It is only after Stonehenge was finished, with the big stones dragged from Avebury, that we see graves that look as though they might have been made for kings: big round barrows containing single burials. Maybe communities like those living at Stonehenge and Avebury competed with each other to see which could make the most spectacular monuments, and their chiefs acquired power in consequence. The chief of the Stonehenge people might then have emerged as Paramount Chief of the Wessex chalklands. Whatever the scenario, the first evidence we have of kings in Britain comes from this time, 2500–2000 BC. It seems unlikely that we shall ever know their names.

The Duggleby Howe King

reigned about 2500 BC

✠

Towards the end of the neolithic, some round barrows were built to honor individual high-status men, probably chiefs. Duggleby Howe in the Yorkshire Wolds is a large round barrow 36 meters across, built of 5000 tonnes of chalk, and surrounded by a huge circular enclosure 300 meters in diameter, the same size as the Great Stone Circle at Avebury. The Duggleby Howe King was buried in a square grave pit covered by a wooden mortuary house. This powerfully built 50-year-old was accompanied to the other world by a boy and an infant; both had been pole-axed. A later burial of another king was similarly accompanied by a boy and a very young child, and this suggests that the sacrifice of children formed part of the funeral rite of a northern king in those days.

The Hove Barrow King

reigned about 2000 BC

❧

A handful of rich burials in southern England shows that there were kings and possibly queens in the early bronze age. One such king was buried under a huge round barrow, said to have been 60 meters across, at Hove in Sussex. He was buried with incredibly valuable objects that only the most powerful families could have acquired. The Hove Barrow King had a beautiful orange-brown cup carved out of a single lump of amber, probably imported from Denmark – and certainly priceless. His body and his possessions, including a bronze dagger and a stone axe, were buried in an oak coffin. The barrow was destroyed in 1856 to make way for housing; its site is now occupied by the back garden of 13 Palmeira Avenue, Hove.

The Bush Barrow King

reigned about 2000 BC

❧

The Bush Barrow King was buried very close to Stonehenge in Wiltshire on a low ridge just south of the stone circle. He had a fine dagger and a diamond-shaped breastplate made out of a sheet of gold; a smaller piece of gold was fixed to his helmet; he also held a scepter: a stone mace-head mounted on a wooden shaft decorated with zig-zag bone fittings. Both the Hove Barrow and Bush Barrow kings were buried under large round barrows. It is tempting to see these wealthy chieftains as kings of Sussex and Wessex at the time the big stones were being raised at Stonehenge, around 2500–2000 BC, but there is no way of knowing whether Sussex or Wessex existed as political units then, and no way of knowing how far the kingdoms stretched.

The Roman and Romano-British Rulers

Cartimandua
reigned about 50–69

By around 50 BC, the Romans were reporting and recording the existence – and even names – of both male and female rulers of the iron age tribes in Britain. After Julius Caesar's reconnaissance expedition in 55 BC, several British kings became Roman allies, enjoying many of the fruits of Roman civilization and preparing the way for the successful Roman invasion of AD 43. The Brigantes tribe commanded the biggest single territory in Britain and dominated the north of England. The complete king list has not survived, but successive rulers included Volisios, Dumnocoveros and the famous Queen Cartimandua, who was pro-Roman and reigned from roughly AD 50 to 69.

Commius

reigned first century BC

The Atrebates tribe living in Hampshire and Sussex changed sides. One of the earlier rulers, Commius, fought against Julius Caesar in Gaul (France) and escaped to Britain. Commius's sons Tincommius, Verica and Epillus divided the kingdom, produced coins on the Roman model and used the title *rex* (king). In the complex warring among the British kingdoms, Verica lost Calleva (Silchester) to the great king Cunobelinus and fled from Sussex to get help from Rome.

Caswallon
reigned first century BC

❧

The Catuvellauni, a powerful tribe living in Hertfordshire, was ruled by King Caswallon (turned into the Latin *Cassivellaunus* by Julius Caesar). Caswallon was aggressive, warlike, and succeeded in uniting several tribes in south-eastern England to make an Eastern Kingdom that could withstand the threatened Roman invasion.

Caesar made straight for Caswallon's heartland, with its capital at St Albans, seeing the British war-leader as his main opponent. Caswallon tried to make the ford across the Thames near Kingston impassable by driving lots of stakes into the mud, but the Roman troops crossed the Thames without too much difficulty. Caswallon was responsible for leading a spirited and heroic resistance to Caesar's second invasion in 54 BC, and is credited with causing the Romans to withdraw in defeat. It would be almost a century before the Romans returned.

Caswallon was succeeded by Androco and

Tasciovanus, who was recognized as king by the Roman emperor Augustus in about 15 BC and who died in AD 10. Androco and Tasciovanus were probably Caswallon's sons.

Cunobelinus

reigned first century AD

Cunobelinus was the pre-eminent British ruler at the time of Christ. He was Tasciovanus's son, a member of the Catuvellauni tribe and a powerful Roman ally. Cunobelinus moved his capital and mint from St Albans (*Verulamium*) to Colchester (*Camulodunum*), another great city of the Eastern Kingdom. He had a daunting reputation as a war-leader and Rome wisely watched and waited until he died before launching a major invasion of Britain. Cunobelinus's son Adminius fled to Rome even before his father died in 43. The Roman historian Suetonius described Cunobelinus as *rex Britannorum*, King of the Britons, which gives an idea of his status among the British kings of the first century. Shakespeare's Cymbeline is loosely based on him.

Caradoc or Caratacus
reigned first century AD

Luckily, Cunobelinus had two more sons, Caradoc (known to the Romans as *Caratacus*) and Togodumnus, who stoutly resisted the Roman invasion. Togodumnus was probably mortally wounded at the Battle of the Medway (43). His brother Caradoc went on with the heroic rearguard action against the advancing Roman armies in southern England and Wales for another four years before he was totally defeated near Ludlow by a Roman army under Ostorius.

After this he fled to the north to take sanctuary with the Brigantes, but this was a bad miscalculation. The Brigantian queen Cartimandua betrayed him to the Romans, who in 51 took him in chains to Rome. So impressed were the Romans by Caradoc's fearlessness and dignity during the humiliating ordeal of the triumph that instead of being put to death he and his family were allowed by the Emperor Claudius to live in comfortable retirement in Rome – a rare example of Roman leniency. Caradoc is thought to have died in about 54.

Cogidubnus

reigned first century AD

❧

The Regni, a sub-group of the Atrebates in West Sussex, had a king who was a Roman ally called Cogidubnus. His capital was *Noviomagus Regnensium* (Chichester). He gave the Roman general Vespasian crucial help in providing a base with a harbor for the invasion of Wessex (where the native Durotriges tribesmen were fiercely hostile to Rome). After the completion of the conquest, Vespasian rewarded Cogidubnus with a great fortune, and Cogidubnus used this to build himself a huge Roman-style palace at Fishbourne near Chichester.

Claudius
reigned 43–54

Roman rule in Britain began in 43. As a province of the Roman Empire, Britain was ruled by the emperor. The Emperor Claudius, who ordered the invasion of Britain, paid a triumphal 16-day visit to his new province. Initially, the client-kings (allies of Rome) were allowed to rule under the emperor.

Boudicca

reigned 60–1

The Iceni, living in East Anglia, initially collaborated with the Romans, under their King Prasutagus, who shrewdly made the Roman emperor Nero his co-heir. But when he died in AD 60, Roman soldiers seized all his lands, pillaged them, flogged Boudicca and raped her daughters. This unexpected and entirely unprovoked outrage caused Boudicca, now an impressive warrior-queen of mature years, with red hair and a harsh voice, to launch a great rebellion against the Romans.

Boudicca made an alliance with the Trinovantes tribe (Essex) and led a successful attack on the Roman garrison town of *Camulodunum* (Colchester), which she destroyed in 60, putting all the settlers to death. She pressed south-west to attack *Verulamium* (St Albans) and the important fortified river-crossing at *Londinium* (London), which she also sacked and burned. It is estimated that 70,000 Roman soldiers were killed.

In 61, Suetonius Paulinus, Roman governor of Britain, returned from Wales, gathered two legions to deal with the rising and routed the Iceni. Boudicca and her Iceni warriors fled north along Watling Street (the A5) and they were overtaken somewhere in the south midlands, probably near Towcester. Some 80,000 British warriors were massacred, but Boudicca herself managed to stay far enough ahead of her pursuers to take poison; she preferred to commit suicide than be taken prisoner and paraded in Rome as a trophy of war. Though she reigned for only one turbulent year, Boudicca is firmly imprinted on British folk-memory as an icon of heroic resistance to invasion.

Marcus Aurelius Carausius
reigned 287–93

❧

Carausius was commander of the British navy, the *Classis Britannica*, and probably the architect of the new Saxon Shore Forts. In 287, Carausius proclaimed an independent British Empire, with himself as its emperor. He ruled Britain until he was murdered by his finance minister, Caius Allectus.

Caius Allectus
reigned 293–6

❧

Allectus usurped the British Empire Carausius had founded. In 296 the junior Roman emperor Constantius Chlorus I, who reigned 296–306, invaded Britain, executed Allectus and restored direct Roman rule.

Honorius

reigned 395–423

❧

In Britain, political power increasingly devolved on the native dynasties, as successive Roman emperors became distracted by troubles nearer to Rome. Like Magnus Maximus before him, the imperial pretender Constantine III withdrew troops from Britain to support his imperial claims in Gaul between 407 and 411. In 410, the Emperor Honorius, hemmed in behind Ravenna's marshes where he had been forced to make his headquarters, wrote to the Britons telling them that from then on they were on their own: Rome could no longer defend them. His historic letter dates the end of Roman rule in Britain.

2

✤

The Kings of Dark Age Britain

Maelgwn
reigned 517–about 550

Maelgwn's dark age kingdom of Gwynedd corresponds roughly with the modern county of Gwynedd in north-west Wales, including Anglesey. Maelgwn's stronghold was Castell Degannwy, not far from Conwy. His great-grandfather was the legendary Cunedda, who was sent from his native Gododdin territory (south-east Scotland) to expel the Irish incomers who had begun to settle in north-west Wales. Maelgwn's grandfather was Enniaun Girt and his father was Caswallon Law Hir. Maelgwn had a son, called Rhun, by his concubine Gwalltwen.

Maelgwn was one of the most powerful kings of Britain. He became *dux bellorum* (commander-in-chief of the Britons) after Arthur's death at the Battle of Camlann. The fact that this last battle of Arthur's took place at a river crossing near Dolgellau, on the southern frontier of Maelgwn's kingdom, suggests that Arthur may have been treacherously ambushed by Maelgwn. Maelgwn was ambitious and ruthless, capable of killing for the honor of becoming British commander-in-chief. He died of plague.

Urien

reigned sixth century

Owain was succeeded as King of Rheged (Cumbria) by Urien son of Cynfach, called "King of the Golden North" by his eloquent and soulful bard Taliesin. Urien was remembered as a great warrior. He was also a pagan king; paganism and Christianity lived uneasily side by side in the sixth century. While out on a campaign in 590 Urien was assassinated at the instigation of his ally Morcant, apparently out of jealousy for Urien's all-surpassing generalship. Morcant commissioned Dyfnwal ap Mynyddawg and Llovan Llawddino of Din Eidyn (Edinburgh) to murder Urien. Owain succeeded to the throne of Rheged.

Geraint

reigned sixth century

The kingdom of Dumnonia consisted of Cornwall, Devon, Somerset and part of Dorset. It was divided into several sub-kingdoms, so there were at any time several kings. One of the royal dynasties can be partially reconstructed back to a patriarch called Erbin. He held lands in both Dumnonia and south-east Wales and when he was too old to rule all his territories he handed over his kingdom in Dumnonia to his son Geraint. Geraint the Fleet-owner was a contemporary of King Arthur, and fought at his side in battle. Geraint seems to have had four sons: Cado (or Cato), Selyf, Cyngar and Iestyn.

Mark
reigned sixth century

Another Dumnonian dynasty was that of King Mark or Cynfawr (Latin form *Conomorus*), whose kingdom centered on Castle Dore, though he also held lands in Brittany. According to an inscription on the Tristan Stone, which stands on the roadside near Castle Dore, Mark's son was Tristan (Latin form *Drustanus*). The romantic story of forbidden love between Tristan and Iseult, and Tristan's betrayal of King Mark's trust, is probably rooted in a real dark age family tragedy. Mark's successor as king was his son Constantine; possibly it was Constantine who raised the memorial to his disgraced brother after their father died.

Arthur
reigned about 516–37

By tradition, and increasingly supported by archaeology, King Arthur (Latin form *Arturus*) also came from a Dumnonian royal dynasty. His kingdom was probably Trigg (Latin form *Tricorium*) and his royal stronghold was Tintagel.

Arthur fought at the Battle of Badon, which was a great victory for the Britons, who stopped the Saxons at Bath and halted the westward expansion of the Saxons for several decades. Ambrosius Aurelianus seems to have been the British commander-in-chief at Badon, though the victory was later counted as the first of Arthur's battles; it may be his conduct in this battle that won him the role of *dux bellorum*.

Arthur is remembered as a great warrior, a charismatic Christian king, a champion of justice, but above all the British champion and overking who held the Saxons back. His mysterious disappearance after the Battle of Camlann (probably fought at Ganllwyd near Dolgellau in 537) is best explained by his abdication and retirement to a remote monastery, possibly Whithorn in southern Scotland. His distraught subjects in Dumnonia may well have hung on to the hope that, one day, he would return. Early in the twelfth century people in Bodmin in Cornwall certainly believed that Arthur was still alive. The alternative tradition Geoffrey of Monmouth got hold of, that King Arthur died in 542, is more likely to be true.

Rhydderch

reigned sixth century

❧

King Dyfnwal (early form of Donald) of Clyde was
succeeded by Rhydderch Hael who owned a special
sword named Dyrnwyn, that was alleged to flame like
fire when unsheathed. Rhydderch was remembered as
a great king and a champion of Christianity. He
supported the mission of the much-loved St
Kentigern.

3

✠

The Anglo-Saxon Kings

Kings of Kent

❦

Hengist reigned about 455–88

Aesc (Oisc) reigned about 488–512

Octa reigned about 512–40

Eormenric reigned about 540–60

Ethelbert I reigned about 560–616

Eadbald reigned 616–40

Earconbert reigned 640–64

Egbert I reigned 664–73

Hlothere reigned 673–85

Eadric reigned 685–7

Oswini reigned 688–90 (jointly with **Suaebhard**)

Wihtred reigned 690–725 (jointly with **Suaebhard**)

Ethelbert II reigned 725–62 (jointly with **Eadbert I, Alric** and **Eardwulf**)

Egbert II reigned about 765–80

𝕰𝖆𝖑𝖍𝖒𝖚𝖓𝖉   reigned about 780–96
𝕰𝖆𝖉𝖇𝖊𝖗𝖙 𝕀𝕀   reigned 796–8

Hengest

reigned about 455–88

❧

The southern British overking Vortigern commissioned Jutish mercenaries to help him fight off his northern enemies, offering them land – the Isle of Thanet – in exchange for military service. Led by the brothers Hengest and Horsa, they landed at Ebbsfleet in Kent (449) and rapidly became an additional threat to Vortigern's security. At a battle with the British beside the Medway river crossing at Aylesford, Horsa met his death (455), but the Jutish army under Hengest quickly established a Jutish territory in Kent. Hengest was the first Jutish King of Kent.

Kings of Sussex

Aelle   reigned about 477–514
Cissa   reigned 514–
Ethelwalh   reigned about 670–85
Berhtun   reigned 685–6
Cadwalla of Wessex   reigned 686–8
Nothelm   reigned 692
Nunna   reigned about 710–25
Aldwuf   reigned about 760–5
Osmund   reigned about 765–70

Aelle
reigned 477–514

❧

Aelle was a Saxon chief who landed with a small number of settlers on the Sussex coast to found a colony. Aelle conquered the coastal plain first, then advanced east, crossing the Sussex Ouse at Seaford, where he fought a great battle against the British, the Battle of Mearcredesburna. After this victory, he pressed east and laid siege to the Saxon Shore Fort of Anderida at Pevensey. The Britons of the area had taken shelter inside the still-imposing Roman walls, but Aelle broke in and killed them all (491). His military tactics won him not only the kingdom of the South Saxons, but the title Bretwalda, "King of Britain." This was the Anglo-Saxon equivalent in rank of the *dux bellorum* of the Britons. In this role he probably co-ordinated, and led into battle, the Anglo-Saxon armies which joined battle with the British under first Ambrosius Aurelianus and later King Arthur. Nothing is known of Aelle's character or personal life; in historic terms he is as shadowy a figure as Arthur, though without the benefit of folk-lore and legend added after his death.

Kings of Essex

❧

Aescwine   reigned about 527–87

Sledda   reigned about 587–603

Saebert   reigned about 603–16

Sexred and **Saeward**   reigned 616–17

Sighebert I the Little   reigned about
    617–before 653

Sighebert II the Good reigned about 653–60

Swithelm   reigned about 660–5

Sighere   reigned about 665–83

Sebbi   reigned about 665–95, jointly with
    Sighere

Sigeheard   reigned about 695–before 709

Offa   reigned in 709

Saelred   reigned 709–46

Swithred   reigned 746–58

Sigeric   reigned 758–98

Sigered   reigned 798–825

Kings of East Anglia

❧

Wuffa   reigned about 571–8

Tytila   reigned about 578–93

Redwald   reigned about 593–617

Eorpwald   reigned about 617–27

Sigeberht   reigned about 631–4

Ecgric   reigned about 634–5

Anna   reigned about 635–54

Ethelhere   reigned 654

Ethelwold   reigned 654–63

Aldwulf   reigned 663–713

Aelfwald   reigned about 713–49

Hun Beonna   reigned about 749

St Ethelbert   reigned 792

Athelstan I   reigned about 828–37

Ethelweard   reigned about 837–50

St Edmund   reigned about 850–70

Redwald

reigned about 593–617

❦

This pagan King of East Anglia was a Wuffing, the grandson of Wuffa, first Anglo-Saxon King of East Anglia (reigned 571–8), with a royal palace at Rendlesham near Ipswich. Redwald was converted to Christianity in Kent by St Augustine, but later converted back to paganism by his wife. He was foster-father to the disinherited young Northumbrian prince Edwin, whom he rescued from assassination. Either by military might or by seniority among the Anglo-Saxon kings, he became the fourth Bretwalda and, in 617, when Edwin had come of age, sent troops to help the young prince regain the Northumbrian throne. Redwald died shortly afterwards and is believed to have been buried in the famous ship burial at Sutton Hoo, the Anglian royal cemetery not far from Ipswich.

St Edmund
reigned about 855–70

❧

Born in about 841, Edmund had the misfortune to be the last Anglo-Saxon King of East Anglia. During his reign, in 865, a great Danish invasion army descended upon East Anglia. Edmund met the Danes in battle at Haegelisdun, near Hoxne in Suffolk, where he was defeated and taken captive. When he refused to renounce his Christian faith, the Danes tied him to a tree and shot him with arrows. After his death a miracle cult quickly developed at Hoxne. His body was eventually dug up in 903 and reburied at Beadoricesworth, later known as Bury St Edmunds, and St Edmund, as he now was, became the patron saint of England until the (inexplicable) adoption of the non-English St George.

Kings of Mercia

Creoda   reigned about 585–93
Pybba   reigned about 593–606
Ceorl   reigned about 606–26
Penda   reigned 632–55
Wulfhere   reigned 657–75
Ethelred   reigned 675–704
Coenred   reigned 704–9
Ceolred   reigned 709–16
Ethelbald   reigned 716–57
Beonred   reigned 757
Offa   reigned 757–96
Egfrith   reigned 796
Coenwulf   reigned 796–821
Ceolwulf I   reigned 821–3
Beornwulf   reigned 825
Ludeca   reigned 827
Wiglaf   reigned 827–40

Beortwulf reigned 840–52
Burgred reigned 852–74
Ceolwulf II reigned 874–80

Penda

reigned 632–55

Before claiming the throne of the midland Anglo-Saxon kingdom of Mercia, Penda had already defeated the West Saxons at Cirencester (628) and annexed the kingdom of Hwicce, which comprised the lower Severn valley. After acceding to the throne of Mercia at the age of 56, Penda formed an alliance with the British king Cadwallada of Gwynedd to defeat the Northumbrians under their great Christian king Oswald at Maserfield (Oswestry) on 5 August 641 – Oswald himself died in the battle – and almost succeeded in capturing Bamburgh Castle, the Northumbrian royal citadel. In 653 he created the sub-kingdom of Middle Anglia in the east midlands, for his son Peada to rule, though Peada died in 656. Another of Penda's sons, Merewald, was made sub-king of the newly conquered Herefordshire.

King Penda finally came to grief when invading Northumbria again. He met the Northumbrian army under King Oswiu beside the flooding River Winwaed near Leeds, refused a peace offering and was defeated and killed. He was nearly 80 years old. Penda was the archetypal Anglo-Saxon warrior-king in the old heroic mold.

Ethelbald
reigned 716–57

Ethelbald inherited the kingdom of Mercia as the grandson of Penda's brother Eowa, who died in 641. He greatly enhanced Mercian power and status during his reign, which at 41 years was the longest in the dynasty. His great achievement was the annexation of Berkshire on Mercia's southern border. He was probably responsible for ordering the building of Wat's Dyke, to defend Mercia against the Welsh. Ethelbald's personal status grew and grew, to the point where he was formally referred to as "King of Britain," though he was never really quite this. King Ethelbald was murdered in 757 by his own retainers at Seckington in Warwickshire and buried at Repton in Derbyshire.

Offa

reigned 757–96

Offa was descended from Penda's youngest brother, and was responsible for consolidating Mercian domination of the whole of England south of the Humber. He styled himself *rex anglorum*, King of the English, which says much about his status and ambition. His queen was Cynethryth; two of their daughters married kings who were Mercian allies.

This great king issued the first major royal coinage ever produced in Britain, putting millions of silver pennies into circulation, and compiled influential laws. He built the great defensive earthwork that bears his name, Offa's Dyke, a barrier 120 miles long to keep the Welsh out, and in 796 made a treaty with

Charlemagne, whom he considered his royal equal. Plans were laid for Offa's daughter to marry one of Charlemagne's sons, but they came to nothing because Charlemagne refused to let one of *his* daughters marry Offa's son Ecgfrith; in fact Charlemagne refused to let any of his daughters marry anyone, but Offa felt snubbed. In many ways he was ahead of his time, setting standards that were more like those of late medieval kings. To ensure the succession, he had his son Ecgfrith anointed king in 787. The two co-ruled for the remainder of Offa's life, but Ecgfrith only survived him by a few months, both father and son dying in 796.

Kings of Northumbria

The kingdom of Northumbria, or Nortanhymbre (Old English "People north of the Humber"), evolved from the fusion of two pre-existing British kingdoms, Bernicia (Northumberland) and Deira (Humberside).

Ida   (first Saxon ruler) reigned about 547
Aelle   ruled Deira about 560–88
Ethelric   ruled Bernicia 568–72
Ethelfrith   ruled Bernicia 592–616
Edwin   reigned 616–33
Eanfrith   reigned 633–4
Oswald I   reigned 634–41
Oswy   reigned 641–70
Egfrith   reigned 670–85
Aldfrith   reigned 685–704
Osred   reigned 704–16
Coenred   reigned 716–18

Osric   reigned 718–29

Ceolwulf   reigned 729–37

Eadbert   reigned 737–58

Oswulf   reigned 758–9

Ethelwald Moll   reigned 759–65

Alhred   reigned 765–74

Ethelred I   reigned 774–8 and 790–6

Elfwald I   reigned 778–88

Osred II   reigned 788–90

Osbald   reigned 796

Eardwulf   reigned 796–808 and 809

Elfwald II   reigned 808–9

Eanred   reigned 809–41

Ethelred II   reigned 841–50

Osberht   reigned 850–63

Aelle   reigned 863–7

Egbert I   reigned 867–72

Ricsig   reigned 872–6

Egbert II   reigned 876–8 (last Viking puppet king)

Edwin

reigned 616–33

Edwin was born in about 585, the son of Aelle, King of Deira. When his father died in 588, Edwin was only three years old and his kingdom was seized by the King of Bernicia. Edwin was taken for safety to the court of King Redwald of East Anglia. Eventually, in 616, Edwin was able to regain his own kingdom and Bernicia as well, effectively uniting Northumbria, when with Redwald's assistance he overpowered and killed King Ethelfrith beside the River Idle. Edwin was a great warlord and empire-builder who became the fifth Bretwalda. He annexed the Isle of Man, Lindsey in Lincolnshire, and the Pennine kingdom of Elmet. When Redwald died in about 625 he assumed overlordship of East Anglia too. Also in 625 he made a significant marriage with Princess Ethelburga of Kent, recently converted to Christianity, and she took a chaplain, Paulinus, with her to Northumbria.

On Easter Day 626, an assassin in the guise of an

envoy from King Cwichelm of Wessex managed to gain audience with Edwin on the pretense of delivering a message. Suddenly he lunged at Edwin and tried to stab him, but a quick-witted courtier called Lilla jumped between them so that the king was only wounded. The incident prompted Edwin and all his court to be converted to Christianity the next year, after first vengefully devastating Wessex; Edwin was sure Christian prayer had saved him.

Edwin died in battle in 633 at Hatfield Chase, his army defeated by a combined force of Welsh and Mercian troops under Cadwallon and Penda, who afterwards burnt the Northumbrian palace at Yeavering.

Oswald

reigned 634–41

❧

Oswald was born about 605, the second son of King Ethelfrith of Bernicia, the brother of King Eanfrith. He was forced to flee from Northumbria when Edwin returned to claim his kingdom from Ethelfrith; he took refuge on Iona in the Hebrides for the duration of Edwin's reign.

On Edwin's death, he returned and fought his way back to the throne by defeating Cadwallon's army at Hexham in 634. He became sixth Bretwalda. He summoned the British monk Aidan from Iona and installed him on Lindisfarne Island, near the royal stronghold of Bamburgh. Both Aidan and Oswald were later canonized for their roles in re-establishing Christianity in Northumbria: Oswald was the first canonized Anglo-Saxon king. Oswald died in the Battle of Maserfield against the pagan Penda of Mercia.

Oswy
reigned 641–70

Oswald's brother, born in about 602, ruled Bernicia for 13 years in the shadow of Penda of Mercia, but went on to annexe Mercia, much of southern Scotland (the old British kingdoms of Rheged and Gododdin) and received the accolade of Bretwalda – the seventh king to hold the title. His secular supremacy was supreme; so too was his spiritual power, as he presided over the all-important Synod of Whitby in 664, at which Northumbria gave up the Church of Iona in favor of Rome.

Kings and Queens of Wessex

❧

Cerdic reigned 519–34
Cynric reigned 534–60
Ceawlin reigned 560–91
Ceol reigned 591–7
Ceolwulf reigned 597–611
Cynegils reigned 611–43
Cenwalh reigned 643–72
Seaxburgh reigned 672–4 (the only Anglo-Saxon queen to reign alone)
Cenfus reigned 674
Aescwine reigned 674–6
Centwine reigned 676–85
Cadwalla reigned 685–8
Ine reigned 688–726

Ethelheard   reigned 726–40

Cuthred   reigned 740–56

Sigeberht   reigned 756–7

Cynewulf   reigned 757–86

Beohrtric   reigned 786–802

Egbert   reigned 802–39

Ethelwulf   reigned 839–58

Ethelbald   reigned 858–60

Ethelbert   reigned 860–5

Ethelred I reigned 865–71
Alfred the Great reigned 871–99

Edward the Elder reigned 899–924

Cerdic

reigned 519–34

The kingdom of the West Saxons was founded in about 494, probably by South Saxon pioneers sent into Hampshire in five ships by King Aelle to extend the newly founded kingdom of Sussex. Cerdic was the first Saxon King of Wessex, and he had to fight his way ashore at a place called Cerdic's Shore, probably on Southampton Water, with a small company of Saxons including his son and heir Cynric.

The British sub-kings of Hampshire were defeated one by one; the British king Nataleod was killed in battle in 508. Cerdic was roundly defeated by the British under Arthur at the Battle of Badon in 516, which contained his territorial ambitions, but Cerdic consolidated his gains and became King of Wessex in 519. Later on, in 530, he conquered the Isle of Wight.

Ceawlin
reigned 560–91

❧

Ceawlin (modern equivalent = Colin) was the grandson of the tribal patriarch Cerdic, and the son of Cynric. Ceawlin was a great war-leader who had the advantage of living in the post-Arthurian period; expansion now became possible, and Ceawlin extended the kingdom of Wessex well beyond Hampshire, advancing north into the Thames valley.

Such was Ceawlin's reputation that he became the second Bretwalda or overking of the Anglo-Saxons. In 568 he defeated Ethelbert of Kent. Then in 577 he won a momentous victory in the Severn valley at the Battle of Dyrham, taking three British sub-kingdoms in one go and killing their kings: Conmail, Condidan and Farinmail. In spite of these great victories, Ceawlin's reign ended with rebellion. He was deposed in 591 and died in exile two years afterwards.

Ine

reigned 688–726

❧

Cerdic and Ceawlin were great rulers: Ine was more powerful than either. He issued the first code of West Saxon laws in 690–3, fought against the Dumnonians (710), fought and defeated the South Saxons (722–5), established Southampton as a port and founded the monastery at Glastonbury.

A Christian king, Ine installed a bishop in Dorset once his troops had defeated the pagan Britons there. Following the custom of the time, he abdicated when increasing age made fighting and incessant campaigning difficult, and followed the religious life. He nevertheless had to be persuaded to do this by his queen, who stage managed a happening at one of the royal palaces. She arranged for cattle to be herded into the hall and a sow to be put into the royal bed. Ine was surprised at this, but the queen preached a powerful sermon on the vanity of royal power, and he gave up his throne. He died on pilgrimage to Rome, just as his predecessor, Cadwalla, had before him.

4

✠

The Kings of England

924–1066

The Saxon Kings

Athelstan
reigned 924–39

Athelstan was the firstborn son of Edward the Elder and Egwina (or Ecgwyn), born in about 895. He succeeded to the English throne on 17 July 924 and was crowned at Kingston-upon-Thames on 4 September 925. His reign was a landmark in English history because he became the first Saxon king to gain effective control over the whole of England, with the exception of Cumbria. He also became nominal overlord of Cornwall, Wales and Scotland.

Athelstan's most spectacular victory was the Battle of Brunanburh (937). King Constantine of the Scots attacked Athelstan's army (a full levy of troops from Wessex and Mercia) with an enormous host of combined Picts, Scots and all the Vikings of the north and west; in this unusually large-scale, all-day, battle *five* kings were slaughtered. After this, neither Scots nor Danes gave the English any more trouble during Athelstan's reign.

Athelstan was a great administrator, introducing a national coinage and passing laws to relieve poverty and punish corruption. He also assembled a team of clerks to help with the administration and thus can be said to have founded the Civil Service. Unusually, he remained unmarried. Athelstan died on 27 October 939 and was buried at Malmesbury Abbey in Wiltshire.

Edmund I

reigned 939–46

❧

Edmund was born in 921, the eldest son of Edward the Elder and Edgifu. He succeeded to the English throne on 27 October 939. After commanding the army at the Battle of Brunanburh under his half-brother King Athelstan, Edmund recaptured areas of the midlands (in 942) and Northumbria (in 944) taken by King Olaf Guthfrithson of Dublin after Athelstan died. His powerful ealdormen West Saxon brothers ruled Kent and East Anglia on his behalf.

Edmund married twice – St Alfifu (died in 944) and Ethelfled – and had two sons, Edwy and Edgar. Edmund was stabbed to death by Leofa, an exiled thief, at Pucklechurch in Gloucestershire on 26 May 946, and was buried in Glastonbury Abbey. He was nicknamed The Deed-Doer, The Elder, The Magnificent.

Edred

reigned 946–55

❧

Edred was born in 923, the second son of Edward the Elder and Edgifu. In spite of ill health, he managed to quell a revolt in the north. His main achievement was to make Northumbria a permanent part of England. When the Northumbrians tried to reject him in favor of the Norwegian Eric Bloodaxe, Edred ravaged their lands and burnt Ripon (948), but the revolt only ended with Bloodaxe's expulsion. Edred's chief adviser was Abbot Dunstan of Glastonbury.

Edwy the Fair

reigned 955–9

❧

Edwy, the eldest son of Edmund I and Elgifu, was born in about 940. Edwy succeeded to the throne too young. At the age of 15, he showed little judgment, quarreling immediately with Dunstan. Dunstan's biographer explained how it happened. "A certain woman pursued the king, wickedly enticing him to intimacy in order to ally herself and her daughter to him in marriage. Shameful to relate, he acted wantonly with them in disgraceful caresses." After his coronation, Edwy withdrew early from the celebration banquet to have sex with the two women. Dunstan and a kinsman went to fetch him. "They found the crown carelessly thrown on the floor and he himself repeatedly wallowing between the two of them in evil fashion, as if in a vile sty." Dunstan pulled him out. Edwy did in fact marry the younger of the two women, Aelgifu, and Dunstan was exiled for interfering.

In 957, Mercia and Northumbria rejected Edwy's

leadership in favor of his younger brother Edgar; after that he ruled only Kent and Wessex. Edwy died on 1 October 959, at the age of 19.

Edgar
reigned 959–75

Though he succeeded to the throne of England in
959, Edgar was not crowned until May 973 (at
Bath). He had two wives, Ethelfled and Elfrida, by
whom he had three children (Edward the Martyr,
Edmund Atheling and Ethelred II); he also had a
mistress, a nun called Wilfthryth, by whom he had a
daughter, St Eadgyth.

Edgar reunited England and reinstated Dunstan
as chief adviser, making him Archbishop of
Canterbury. Edgar built a navy to consolidate his
peaceable hold on England, and received homage

from the kings of Strathclyde and Scotland. After his coronation he was rowed on the River Dee by eight kings in a spectacular but characteristically peaceful display of his supremacy; the kings were Malcolm of Strathclyde, Kenneth II of Scotland, Maccus of Man and five Welsh kings.

Edward II (the Martyr)

reigned 975–8

❦

Sometimes known as St Edward or Edward the Martyr, Edward II was only 12 when he acceded to the throne of England on 8 July 975. Edward supported his adviser Dunstan, but failed to prevent the widespread expulsion of monks from monastic estates by powerful barons. On a visit to Corfe Castle on 18 March 978, Edward was stabbed to death at the castle gate at his step-mother's orders, so that her son Ethelred would inherit the throne. He was buried first at Wareham, then (980) at Shaftesbury Abbey. Miracles reported at his tomb led to his being venerated as a martyr and saint from 1001.

Ethelred II (the Unready)
reigned 978–1016

Ethelred the Unready, the second son of Edgar I and Elfrida, was born in 968. He was crowned King of England (at the tender age of ten) at the traditional Saxon crowning place, Kingston-upon-Thames, on 11 April 978. He married twice: Elfled of Northumbria and Emma of Normandy, by whom he had at least eight children, one of whom was Edward the Confessor.

Ethelred reigned an incredible 38 years, in spite of the fact that he was an incompetent strategist and militarist. He failed to buy off the Viking raiders who relentlessly raided the English coasts from 980 onwards. He levied taxes to raise the huge sums of protection money he in vain paid to the Vikings. In desperation, he ordered the massacre of Danish settlers throughout England on 13 November 1002. This provoked invasions by the Danish king Sweyn (1003–6) and Thorkell the Tall (1009–13). In the end, Ethelred fled to Normandy in 1013, returning to England after Sweyn's death in 1014. To this chain of disasters must be added Ethelred's marriage to the daughter of the Duke of Normandy, creating a cross-Channel family tie that was to become the pretext for the 1066 Norman invasion.

Ethelred died in London on 23 April 1016 and was buried in Old St Paul's Cathedral. Ethelred's famous nickname is a modern translation of the Anglo-Saxon "Unraed," which would be better translated "Heedless" – a title he richly deserved.

Edmund II (Ironside)
reigned 1016

The eldest surviving son of Ethelred and Elfed, Edmund was to reign for only seven months, from 23 April to 30 November 1016, when he died. Edmund was a more effective warrior than his father, though in 1015 he had failed to prevent Canute's invasion of Wessex, largely because of the treachery of a Mercian prince. Edmund worked hard in the early months of 1016 to muster an army to hold Northumbria against Canute's aggression. He was further undermined by divisions within the English camp; London and the Witan members living there chose him as king, but the Witan majority at Southampton chose Canute. Edmund marched on Wessex and won three out of four battles. Finally, at Olney, Edmund and Canute agreed on the partition of England. A few weeks later Edmund died, possibly of natural causes, possibly murdered. His infant sons were taken out of the country for safety, settling in Hungary.

The Scandinavian Kings

Sweyn (Sven)
reigned 1013–14

Sweyn Forkbeard was already King of Denmark, seizing it from his father in 987, and of Norway, which he seized in 1000, before he became King of England. He repeatedly attacked the English coast, securing protection money from 994 onwards. The St Brice's Day massacre gave him a reason to attack in earnest; his own sister Gunhild had been murdered. He drove Ethelred from the country and made himself King of England in December. He died only two months later, in Gainsborough, after falling from his horse.

Canute (Cnut or Knut)
reigned 1016–35

Canute founded a Danish dynasty in England. He fought Edmund, the Saxon king, to a point where the Saxons had to agree to a partition of England. Canute proved to be a wise and statesmanlike king. To win over the English, as a gesture of goodwill he sent back to Denmark all the Danes he could spare. He was nevertheless not soft-hearted. In 1028 he conquered Norway and thus became king of three countries, in effect emperor of the North Sea. He gained some sort of overlordship of Scotland and Dublin. He also rigorously stamped out any threat of resistance, by judicial murder.

Canute ruled ably and justly, and spent more time in England than in his other kingdoms. His advisers sycophantically told him he was so great that even the waves would obey him. To show them how foolish this was he ordered his throne to be placed on the shore at low tide, commanded the waves to hold back — and of course the tide came in regardless of his majesty.

He stoutly supported the Church, going on pilgrimage to Rome in 1027–8. Canute died at Shaftesbury on 12 November 1035 and was buried in Winchester Old Minster.

Harold I (Harefoot)
reigned 1035–40

✤

Canute's son Harold was born in 1016, succeeding him in November 1035. Harold ruled in England as Regent, a role to which he was elected in Oxford. In 1036, his followers blinded and murdered his rival claimant to the throne, Edmund Atheling (Ethelred II's son). Even though he was illegitimate, Harold had himself proclaimed King of England in 1037. Harold repulsed invasions by the Scots and Welsh. Harold died at Oxford, after reigning only four years, on 17 March 1040, and was buried in Old Westminster Abbey.

Hardicanute (Harthacnut)

reigned 1040–2

❦

Hardicanute was Canute's second son, born in 1018. His reign was riven by treachery and violence. His half-brother Harold Harefoot briefly deposed him while he, Hardicanute, was establishing his control over Denmark. When Harold died, Hardicanute reappeared in English waters with a huge fleet. He made himself unpopular by several acts of unnecessary violence. He threw Harold's body into a bog, murdered the captured Earl Edwulf of Northumbria, and burnt Worcester for the murder of tax collectors. Hardicanute died of a fit on 8 June 1042, while drinking at a feast at Lambeth. Within two years of succeeding to the throne he was dead and the English throne passed back to the English line: to Edward, son of Ethelred.

The Late Saxon Kings

❧

Edward the Confessor

reigned 1042–66

Edward was born in 1003 at Islip in Oxfordshire, the eldest son of Ethelred II and Emma of Normandy. He was saintly (founding Westminster Abbey) but ineffectual and politically inept. He lived in exile in Normandy during the Danish supremacy in England from 1013 to 1041; when he returned to become king he restored the Saxon royal line but boosted Norman influence. During his reign it was really Earl Godwin who ran England. After a row with Godwin, Edward banished the Godwin family, bringing Normans into prominence at court; it was at this time (1051) that he promised the crown to William of Normandy – arguably an act of treason. The Godwin family returned to favor and after Earl Godwin's death – he choked on a piece of bread – Edward relied heavily on Godwin's son Harold. As he lay dying, Edward named Harold his successor. His canonization in 1161 has overshadowed his poor kingship.

Harold II
reigned 1066

Second son of Godwin and Gytha (a Danish princess), Harold was doomed to reign only nine months from his coronation in Westminster Abbey on 5 January 1066 to his death on the battlefield on 14 October, though in a sense he had ruled England for the previous 12 years. History remembers Harold mainly for losing, but he was a great military leader, adding Hereford to his personal estates and crushing Welsh risings by 1063. It was then he acquired a Welsh wife, Aldgyth, widow of Gruffydd ap Llywelyn, who replaced his mistress, Edith Swan Neck. He had himself declared king on Edward's death, but there were three rival claimants to the throne of England. The first, the 16-year-old Edgar the Atheling, he could afford to ignore, marching north to fend off an invasion by the second contender, Harold Hardrada of Norway, killing both Hardrada and his own brother Tostig at the Battle of Stamford Bridge on 25 September. Then he marched south with an exhausted army to meet the invasion force of the third contender, William of Normandy, at Battle on 14 October. Harold was cut down with swords, not struck in the eye by an arrow; either way, he died and his death ended 600 years of Anglo-Saxon rule. Two of Harold's sons landed in Devon during the 1068–9 rebellion against William, but it is not known what became of them. A story that Harold survived the Battle of Hastings and lived in monastic retreat in Chester was widely believed at the time: it is said that he was visited there by Henry I. The Anglo-Saxon community could not bear to think that he was dead, just as the Britons long before had not wanted to think of Arthur as dead.

5

❦

The Kings and
Queens of Scotland

The Kings of the Picts

❧

Bridei I   reigned 556–86
Gartnart   reigned 586–97
Nectu   reigned 597–
Cinioch   reigned –631
Garnard   reigned 631–5
Bridei II   reigned 635–41
Talorc   reigned 641–53
Talorcen   reigned 653–7
Gartnait   reigned 657–63
Drest I   reigned 663–71
Bridei III   reigned 671–92
Taran   reigned 692–6
Bridei IV   reigned 696–706
Nechton   reigned 706–24
Drest II   reigned 724–6
Alpin I   reigned 726–8
Onuist   reigned 728–61

Bridei V   reigned 761–3

Ciniod   reigned 763–75

Alpin II   reigned 775–80

Drest III   reigned 780–1

Talorcen   reigned 781–5

Talorgen I   reigned 785–7

Canaul   reigned 787–9

Constantine   reigned 789–820

Unuist   reigned 820–34

Drest IV   reigned 834–7

Uen   reigned 837–9

Uurad   reigned 839–42

Bred   reigned 842

Kineth   reigned 842

Brude   reigned 843–5

Drust   reigned 845–8

The House of Fergus and Loarn

❧

Kenneth I Macalpin
reigned 841–58

❧

Kenneth subdued the Picts and so became the first King of the Picts and Scots. His dynasty was the line of Dalriada (Argyll) kings, who had intermarried with the Picts. Kenneth's kingdom, called Alba, included all the lands north of the Firth and Clyde. He moved the church centre from Iona to the mainland: Dunkeld on the River Tay. He had daughters who married King Olaf I of Dublin and the King of Strathclyde. Kenneth prepared the way for a kingdom of Scotland.

Donald I
reigned 858–62

Kenneth was succeeded by his brother Donald.

Constantine I
reigned 862–77

Constantine was another of Kenneth's brothers. His sister married Rhun, the King of Strathclyde; their son Eocha would later become king. Constantine was defeated in battle by Vikings, who afterwards dragged him into a cave where they murdered him in cold blood.

Aedh
reigned 877–8

Also died fighting the Vikings.

Eocha and Giric I
reigned 878–89

Eocha was the nephew of Constantine I. Giric was descended from Donald I. They were deposed in 889.

Donald II

reigned 889–900

Donald II was killed in battle.

Constantine II

reigned 900–42

Constantine II was a descendant of King Aedh. He was the first Scottish king to render homage to an English king, Edward the Elder, in 924, and thus began the long period of Scottish subordination to England. Constantine shared in the great northern defeat at Brunanburh (937), where one of his sons was killed by King Edward's son Athelstan.

Malcolm I

reigned 942–54

Malcolm was killed in battle in 954.

Indulf

reigned 954–62

Indulf's reign ended in abdication in 962.

Duff (Dubh)
reigned 962–6

Duff was killed in battle in 966.

Cuilean
reigned 966–71

Cuilean was killed in 971.

Kenneth II
reigned 971–95

Kenneth was Duff's brother. He obtained Lothian from the English king Edgar. Kenneth was murdered in 995.

Constantine III
reigned 995–7

Constantine was murdered in 997.

Kenneth III
reigned 997–1005

❦

Giric II was Kenneth's son and co-ruler. Kenneth was killed in battle by Malcolm II in 1005.

Malcolm II
reigned 1005–34

❦

Malcolm was the son of Kenneth II and became King of Alba in 1005. He became the first King of all Scotland in 1016 when he made his grandson Duncan king of the ancient kingdom of Strathclyde. He went on to defeat the Northumbrians at Carham (1018) and take in the English-speaking area of south-eastern Scotland and the Brittonic-speaking area of south-western Scotland. His daughter married Sigurd II the Stout, Norse Earl of Orkney.

Duncan I

reigned 1034–40

✣

On his mother's side, Duncan was grandson of
Malcolm II, who chose him as his successor. Duncan's
father was Crinan, Abbot of Dunkeld (hence the
dynasty's new name), and his mother was Bethoc.
Duncan died in battle (not in bed) in 1040 fighting
Macbeth, a rival claimant to the Scottish throne.

Macbeth

reigned 1040–57

𝕸acbeth's claim depended on his membership of the junior royal line of Loarn, his rule of the province of Moray, and his marriage to the granddaughter of Kenneth III. Lady Macbeth's name was Gruach, and she was innocent of Duncan's murder. Macbeth became King of Scotland by killing his cousin Duncan and driving out Duncan's elder sons Malcolm and Donald Bane. It was intervention from England that brought about Macbeth's downfall. Edward the Confessor sent Earl Siward of Northumberland to support Malcolm, and Macbeth was defeated, as Shakespeare has it, at Dunsinane near Scone (1054). The king escaped, was pursued to the north, and killed by Malcolm at Lumphanan in 1057.

Lulach

reigned 1057–8

Macbeth's stepson Lulach became King of Scots for a short time before he too was killed in an ambush in 1058.

The House of Dunkeld

Malcolm III
reigned 1058–93

Malcolm "Canmore" was born in about 1031. His reign opened over two hundred years of unbroken rule by the House of Dunkeld, also known as Canmore (chief). Malcolm was exiled to England during Macbeth's reign. With English help he was able to defeat Macbeth in 1054, and kill him in 1057. After the death of Macbeth's stepson and successor Lulach, Malcolm became King of all Scotland and was crowned on 25 April 1058. Malcolm's first marriage was to Ingibjorg, the widow of Earl Thorfinn of Orkney, and this strengthened ties with the Scandinavian communities of the north of Scotland. His second wife was St Margaret (1045–93), and she helped strengthen ties with the English; her brother was Edgar the Atheling (died 1125), who was a prince with a claim to the English throne. Malcolm verbally acknowledged William the Conqueror as overlord, but this did not stop him trying – five times – to conquer northern England for himself. During his fifth attempt he was killed, and he was buried with his wife, St Margaret, at Dunfermline. One of his daughters married Henry I of England, creating an important dynastic link between the two countries that would eventually lead to union.

Donald III
reigned 1093–May 1094, November 1094–7

Donald Bane, the brother of Malcolm III, was born in about 1031, and succeeded to the throne of Scotland on 13 November 1093. He was opposed by Malcolm's two sons, deposed twice and finally blinded. He was the last king to be buried in the royal cemetery on Iona.

Duncan II

reigned 1094

❧

Duncan II was born in about 1060, the son of
Malcolm III and Ingibjorg. William II of England
helped him to the Scottish throne in May 1094,
deposing his uncle Donald Bane, but Donald killed
him and regained the throne on 12 November 1094.

Edgar

reigned 1097–1107

❧

Edgar was born in about 1074, the son of Malcolm III and Margaret. He acknowledged William II of England as his overlord. In 1098 he gave the Hebrides to Magnus III of Norway. Edgar did not marry.

Alexander I the Fierce
reigned 1107–24

Alexander the Fierce was born in about 1080. He succeeded his elder brother Edgar, but let his younger brother David rule the south (Cumbria, Strathclyde and Lothian). Alexander married Sibylla, illegitimate daughter of Henry I of England, and also joined in Henry I's Welsh campaign in 1114.

David I the Saint
reigned 1124–53

David I was born in about 1084 and succeeded to the throne in April 1124. He was an important king who established a central government, issued the earliest royal coinage in Scotland, and built castles at Berwick, Stirling and Edinburgh. The way he strengthened Anglo-Norman feudal and aristocratic influence showed his background at the English court of Henry I, his brother-in-law. In 1136, King David fought in the English civil war on behalf of his niece Matilda; in doing so he secured parts of Cumbria and Northumberland for himself. David died on 24 May 1153 at Carlisle in Cumbria.

Malcolm IV the Maiden
reigned 1153–65

Malcolm the Maiden was born in 1141, the son of Henry, Earl of Northumberland, and grandson of King David. He was only about 12 years old when he succeeded to the Scottish throne. Malcolm managed to subdue Somerled, Lord of the Isles and founder of the clan MacDonald. He did not marry but left an illegitimate son. Malcolm is thought to have been the last Gaelic-speaking monarch.

Malcolm IV died at Jedburgh Abbey on 9 December 1165.

William I the Lion
reigned 1165–1214

❧

William I was born in about 1143, the younger brother of Malcolm IV. He fought hard to get Northumberland back off the English, initiating the "Auld Alliance" with France against the English in the attempt. He was captured at Alnwick and forced to acknowledge Henry II as his overlord in 1174. He was nevertheless able to buy back Scottish sovereignty from Richard I in return for a £6600 contribution to the Third Crusade. William strengthened central authority and introduced the lion rampant to the royal arms of Scotland. He died at Stirling on 4 December 1214 and was buried at Arbroath Abbey, which he founded.

Alexander II

reigned 1214–49

Alexander II was born at Haddington in East Lothian on 24 August 1198, the son of William the Lion. He successfully asserted control over Argyll, Caithness and Moray, but failed to win back the northern counties of England. With Henry III he agreed the Peace of York (1237), which fixed the border between Scotland and England roughly where it is today. Alexander married twice: first Joan, eldest legitimate daughter of England's King John, then Marie de Coucy of Picardy. Alexander II died on Kerrera Island, Argyll, on 8 July 1249, and was buried at Melrose Abbey.

Alexander III
reigned 1249–86

✤

Alexander III was born on 4 September 1241, and succeeded to the throne on 8 July 1249 at the age of only seven. During his long minority lasting until 1262, he was seized by one court faction after another. Once he was a ruler in his own right, he defeated a Norwegian invasion attempt. He also bought the Hebrides and the Isle of Man from King Magnus VI of Norway (1266) for the princely sum of £2666. Alexander III managed to maintain good relations with England. He even attended the coronation of Edward I, but declined to offer homage. He married twice: first Margaret, daughter of Henry III, second Yolande, daughter of the Comte de Dreux.

Alexander III outlived his daughter and two sons. He was killed on 19 March 1286 when his horse jumped off a cliff during a night ride near Kinghorn.

Margaret "The Maid of Norway"

reigned 1286–90

✤

Margaret was born in 1283, a granddaughter of Alexander III and daughter of King Erik II of Norway (hence her nickname, The Maid of Norway). She was the last of the line of Malcolm III.

She died on about 26 September 1290 in the Orkneys, during a voyage from Norway. At the time of her death she was committed to marrying the English Prince of Wales, the future Edward II. After this, Edward I declared himself overlord of Scotland. An interregnum of two years followed, and many more years of fighting.

John Balliol
reigned 1292–6

❧

John Balliol was born in about 1250, the grandson of David I's eldest daughter. He was chosen by Scotland's self-appointed overlord, Edward I, from among 13 contestants. The Scots rejected Edward's overlordship, and Balliol signed a treaty of alliance with the French. Edward's response to this was to invade Scotland, where he defeated the Scots at the Battle of Dunbar (1296), compelled Balliol to abdicate and seized the Scottish coronation stone as a trophy. A second Scottish interregnum lasted from 1296 to 1306.

Robert I
reigned 1306–29

Robert I was born on 11 July 1274 at Writtle, near Chelmsford – a long way from Scotland. Robert de Bruce VIII, Earl Carrick, now almost always called Robert the Bruce, was great-grandson of David I. Robert seized the Scottish throne after stabbing and killing his rival John Comyn the Red at Dumfries. Comyn was Balliol's nephew. Edward I's troops came looking for him and he went into hiding, but after Edward's death Robert's guerrilla tactics gradually strengthened his position. Robert won the Battle of Bannockburn (1314) against an exhausted English army led by Edward II, and effectively determined Scotland's independence as a nation. He invaded northern England and forced the young Edward III to forgo any claim to Scotland in the Treaty of Northampton (1328).

Robert de Bruce died, possibly of leprosy, on 7 June 1329 and was buried at Dunfermline.

David II
reigned 1329–71 (intermittently)

David II was born on 5 March 1324 at Dunfermline, the only surviving son of Robert I. He became Scotland's first anointed monarch in a ceremony at Scone on 24 November 1331. The contest for the throne nevertheless continued and John Balliol's son Edward Balliol, who was pro-English, forced David into exile in 1334. He returned in 1341. In an attempt to invade England, David was defeated, wounded and captured in 1346, and remained in prison until 1357. He agreed initially to pay a huge ransom in installments, but instead of completing these payments he offered (in 1363) to make an English prince heir to the throne of Scotland.

David II died childless in Edinburgh Castle on 22 February 1371.

Edward Balliol

reigned 1332–41

Edward Balliol was the eldest son of John Balliol, and Edward III's nominee for the Scottish throne. Balliol and other disinherited Scottish lords invaded Scotland with French support, killing David II's Regent, Donald Earl of Mar, on 12 August 1332. Balliol was crowned "Edward I" at Scone, but did not enjoy his kingdom for long. He was defeated by another Scots army in December. Edward III intervened and in return Edward Balliol gave most of the Scottish Lowlands to England (1341), and finally gave up all his claims and lands to Edward III on 21 January 1356.

The House of Stewart

Robert II
reigned 1371–90

Robert II was born on 2 March 1316, the son of Walter the Steward and Robert I's daughter Marjorie. Robert II was the founder of the Stewart (Stuart) dynasty that was later to rule both Scotland and England. His first wife was Elizabeth Mure, who bore him nine children; the second was Euphemia Ross, who gave him two sons and two daughters. Robert also had at least eight illegitimate children. The nickname he acquired in later life, King Blearie, referred to his bloodshot eyes. He died on 19 April 1390 at Dundonald.

Robert III
reigned 1390–1406

Robert III was born (John Stewart) in about 1337, the eldest son of Robert II and Elizabeth Mure. His career as an active king was cut short when he was kicked by a horse and disabled. Power was once more in dispute; Highlanders descended on the Lowlands and rivalry broke out between the king's brother, the Duke of Albany, and his eldest son David, who was murdered in 1402. Robert III died on 4 April 1406 at Rothesay.

James I
reigned 1406–37

James I was born in December 1394, the second son of Robert III. He was captured by the English while sailing to France in 1406 and imprisoned in the Tower (mainly) until 1424. During his long absence, Scotland was ruled by his uncle, Robert, Duke of Albany (who died in 1420), and the duke's son. In prison, James I wrote the famous poem "Kingis Quair" (The King's Book).

After the payment of a ransom James was released and he returned to Scotland. His reign was a difficult one, as he had to contend with a powerful independent aristocracy. He was murdered on 21 February 1437 in his apartments in Perth by Sir Robert Graham during a dispute over the throne. The king's trusted chamberlain, Sir Robert Stuart, let Graham and his followers into the house. His ladies-in-waiting put up a spirited defense, but they were unable to prevent the intruders from killing the king.

James II
reigned 1437–60

James II was born at Holyroodhouse on 16 October 1430, the surviving twin son of James I. He had a large birthmark, which led to his nickname, Fiery Face. He was crowned at Kelso Abbey, the first time the coronation ceremony did not take place at Scone. James traveled energetically and suppressed opponents and so succeeded in strengthening the flagging power of the monarchy. He killed both the eighth and ninth earls of Douglas. He himself was killed on 3 August 1460 when a cannon exploded beside him while he laid siege to Roxburgh. Undeterred, his wife, Mary of Guelders, went on to take the English-held town.

James III
reigned 1460–88

James III was born in May 1452, the eldest son of James II, and succeeded to the throne at the age of eight. His minority lasted until 1469, and he was unable after that to assert his authority.

James married Margaret, daughter of King Christian I of Denmark and Norway; the generous dowry consisted of Orkney, Shetland and the Western Isles. But it was an unlucky reign; he faced two rebellions of nobles backed by his own son, the future James IV. After being wounded and defeated at the Battle of Sauchieburn, close to Bannockburn, James III was caught and murdered on 11 June 1488 by a soldier dressed up as a priest.

James IV
reigned 1488–1513

James IV was born on 17 March 1473, the son of James III, whose downfall he engineered. James IV was a born leader and ruler, full of imaginative ideas: he seemed the best king Scotland had seen for a hundred years. He strengthened the unity of Scotland, suppressing the last Lord of the Isles, John II, in 1493. James built a modern navy. He fought England on behalf of the pretender Perkin Warbeck. He also made a clever dynastic marriage (1503) to Margaret Tudor, the eldest daughter of Henry VII of England. This marriage, producing four sons and two daughters, formed the basis for the Stuart inheritance of England.

James took another opportunity, nevertheless, to take sides against England, fighting with France in 1513. Threatened with excommunication by the pope, and against good advice from courtiers, it was a fatal mistake. He died on 9 September 1513 at the Battle of Flodden, fighting on foot. He was the last British king to fall in battle. It is thought that James IV's body lies buried in the Church of St Michael, Wood Street, in the City of London.

James V

reigned 1513–42

❦

James V was born at Linlithgow on 10 April 1512, the son of James IV. He succeeded to the throne of Scotland at the age of 17 months, and was during his childhood a pawn in the power game between pro-French Catholic and pro-English Protestant factions. Between 1526 and 1528 James was imprisoned by his step-father, Archibald Earl of Angus, but he escaped and asserted his own, pro-French Catholic, authority.

He formed an alliance with France, refused to meet Henry VIII at York, instigated a foolhardy invasion of England, and inevitably provoked a fierce English response – the utter defeat at Solway Moss (1542). After this rout, James V's health broke down completely and he died on 14 December 1542 at Falkland. His two infant sons died before him in 1541 and his daughter, the famous Mary Queen of Scots, was born only a week before his death.

Mary Queen of Scots
reigned 1542–67

❧

Mary Queen of Scots was born at Linlithgow Castle on 7 December 1542, and succeeded to the throne only seven days later. She spent her childhood in Catholic France and married the Dauphin Francis (1558) who later became Francis II. When he died in 1560 Mary returned to Scotland (1561) to marry a cousin, Henry Stewart, Lord Darnley (1565), who was created Duke of Albany and Henry King of Scots. They had a son, who later became James VI.

Darnley became jealous of his wife's fondness for her secretary, David Rizzio, and conspired to have him murdered. Rizzio was dragged from Mary's presence and stabbed to death outside her chamber. This horrific episode was foreshadowed by an earlier incident that was curiously similar. When she was in France, a young French musician called Chatelar used to visit Mary in her chamber and was intimate enough with her to alarm the courtiers. One evening her ladies-in-waiting raised the alarm, Chatelar was seized, tried in secret, condemned to death in secret and executed.

The murder of Rizzio upset Mary deeply and estranged her from Darnley. Shortly afterwards, Darnley was strangled by assassins after an explosion during the night at Kirk o' Field in Edinburgh (1567), probably at the instigation of James, Earl of Bothwell. Bothwell raised suspicions by divorcing his wife and hastily marrying Mary, even though he was a Protestant. How much Mary herself was implicated in the plot to blow up and kill Darnley is not known. The Scottish lords had their suspicions and were outraged by Mary's extraordinary behavior. They imprisoned her and forced her to abdicate in favor of her infant son, the young James VI of Scotland (to become James I of England).

She — unwisely as it turned out — escaped and made her way to England, where she was heir to the throne. Since Elizabeth was still firmly sitting on it, this was a threatening visit. Elizabeth rightly feared pro-Catholic conspiracies to make Mary queen of England and had her imprisoned. Plots centering on Mary were rumored, and one of these led to Mary's trial for treason at Fotheringhay Castle (15 October 1586) and her eventual execution. Elizabeth could not for some time bring herself to sign the death warrant, having traumatic memories of herself being an heir to a throne who was the innocent and unwilling focus of conspiracies. She did nevertheless sign it in the end.

Mary Queen of Scots was executed in the Great Hall of Fotheringhay Castle on 8 February 1587. She was buried first in Peterborough Cathedral, then transferred (1612) by her son James I to Henry VII's Chapel in Westminster Abbey.

6

✦

The Kings and Princes of Wales

Merfyn Frych
(Merfyn the Freckled)
reigned 825–44

❧

Merfyn was King of Gwynedd. He married Nest, the King of Powys's daughter.

Rhodri Mawr (the Great)

reigned 844–78

Rhodri Mawr was King of Gwynedd, the son of Merfyn and Nest. He fought off attacks by Vikings (856) and dominated most of Wales, partly by marrying Angharad, heiress of Greater Ceredigion (Cardigan). He was for a time exiled by Viking invaders, but returned to die in battle against the English Mercians.

Anarawd

reigned 878–916

Anarawd was King of Gwynedd, son of Rhodri Mawr. He shared the rule of Rhodri's extensive kingdom with his five brothers. Anarawd made an alliance with the King of York and raided South Wales. The kings of South Wales appealed to King Alfred of Wessex for help. Anarawd himself paid homage to Alfred, the first time a Welsh king made such a submission. He did this to enlist Alfred's support against his own brother Cadell of Ceredigion.

Hywel Dda the Good
reigned 904–50

❧

Hywel Dda was the son of Cadell and the grandson of Rhodri. He briefly united North and South Wales (942–50). It was by marrying Princess Elen, daughter of the King of Dyfed, that he secured the kingdom of Dyfed (south-west Wales). Later he absorbed Gwynedd and Powys, at the same time acknowledging Edward the Elder (918) and Athelstan (928) as English overlords. Hywel made a pilgrimage to Rome in 928. He was a king of great stature, and was the only Welsh king to issue his own coins (silver pennies).

Iago ap Idwal I

reigned 950–79

❧

Iago was the son of Idwal Foel (Idwal the Bald) and grandson of Anarawd. He was expelled from Gwynedd by Hywel Dda, but after Hywel's death he fought his way back against Owain, Hywel's son. Iago was deposed in 979 by his son, Hywel the Bad.

Hywel ap Idwal the Bad

reigned 979–85

Hywel was King of Gwynedd. He was succeeded by his brother Cadwallon, who reigned 985–6.

Maredudd ap Owain

reigned 986–99

Maredudd was Owain's son, Hywel's grandson. He once more unified Wales, but the union disintegrated on his death in 999.

Cynan
reigned 999–1005

Cynan was the son of Hywel the Bad. He succeeded to the throne of Gwynedd when Maredudd died.

Gruffydd ap Llywelyn

reigned 1039–63

✤

Gruffydd (Griffith son of Llywelyn ap Seisyll) succeeded in conquering Gwynedd and Powys in 1039, briefly uniting Wales by annexing South Wales (1055). He married the daughter of a Mercian earl, and then made the mistake of attacking English lands to the east. This led to counter-attacks from the English. Harold Godwinson (later King Harold II of England) captured his court at Rhuddlan in 1062. Gruffydd's own followers took his severed head as a trophy to Harold, who was to be the last Anglo-Saxon king.

Gruffyd ap Cynan

reigned 1081–1137

Gruffydd belonged to the Gwynedd royal dynasty, though he was born in Ireland. Three times he invaded Gwynedd. He secured it for a short time in 1081 by defeating the King of Powys, Trahaiarn, but he was then captured by the Normans. They took him to Chester, but he escaped and continued the resistance against the Normans during William II's reign. Finally he rendered homage to Henry I.

Owain Gwynedd
reigned 1137–70

❧

Owain was born in about 1100, the son of Gruffydd ap Cynan. He strengthened the kingdom of Gwynedd, extending it both eastwards and south-wards. Henry II forced him to submit in 1157, but Owain formed an alliance with the South Wales rulers to oppose Henry's 1165 campaign. Owain's son Dafydd, who reigned after him (1170–94), married Henry II's half-sister Emma.

Llywelyn ap Iorwerth

reigned 1194–1240

❦

Llywelyn the Great, son of Iorwerth, was born at Dolwyddelan Castle in Gwynedd in 1173. This grandson of Owain Gwynedd defeated his uncle Dafydd who had exiled him, and reunited the fragmented Gwynedd. From this base he dominated other Welsh princes. In 1205, he married Joan, the illegitimate daughter of King John of England. John attempted to curb his power in 1210–11, but Llywelyn reached out and seized several royal castles in South Wales. He achieved formal recognition of his military achievement in 1218, when at Worcester he was declared Wales's paramount lord, taking the title Lord of Snowdon. Llywelyn died at Conwy on 11 April 1240.

David ap Llywelyn
reigned 1240–6

David was the second son but widely recognized heir of Llywelyn ap Iorwerth. He held the title of Prince of Wales from 1244. He died suddenly and unexpectedly without an heir. This led directly to the partition of Wales among the sons of his elder brother.

Llywelyn ap Gruffydd

reigned 1246–82

Llywelyn was the eldest son of Gruffydd, who died while trying to escape from the Tower of London in 1244. Llywelyn the Last became powerful enough to earn the title Prince of Wales, and even received recognition from Henry III of England in 1267. He married Eleanor, daughter of Simon de Montfort in 1278, but she died in childbirth in 1282. Family quarrels weakened Llywelyn's position. He rashly refused to offer homage to Edward I of England; in the war of 1266–7 he lost control of almost all of Wales – only the west of Gwynedd was left. Llywelyn, the last hereditary Welsh Prince of Wales, died in December 1282. His only child, Gwenllian, died in a nunnery at Sempringham in Lincolnshire in 1337.

Owain Glyndwr

reigned 1400–9

❧

Owain Glyndwr was born in about 1355. He was Lord of Glyndwr in North Wales and proclaimed himself Prince of Wales in 1400, after which announcement he led a spectacular rebellion against Henry IV and the rule of the English. His successes reached their peak in 1405, at which time Owain controlled almost the whole of Wales. The fall of Harlech in 1409 effectively marked the end of the revolt, though Owain and his followers went on fighting sporadically for another three years. It is not certain how Owain ended his days. Some say that he received a pardon from the English and lived out a peaceful retirement, dying of natural causes in about 1417.

7

✦

The Kings and Queens of England

1066–1603

The House of Normandy

William I
reigned 1066–87

William the Conqueror was born in Falaise, Normandy, in 1027, the illegitimate son of Robert, Duke of Normandy, by a tanner's daughter called Arlette. When his father died in 1035 the Norman nobles accepted him as duke, but his youth was beset by difficulties and dangers. In 1047 the lords of the western part of his duchy rebelled and he had to be helped by King Henri I of France. Edward the Confessor died childless and William, a cousin of Edward's, claimed that the dead king had promised him the English throne during a visit in 1051; he may well have received such a promise.

The pope approved William's claim to the English throne. William then assembled a fleet, crossed the Channel, and defeated Harold Godwinson on 14 October 1066 near Hastings. He circled London to approach it from the north, meeting relatively little resistance. He had himself crowned in an almost deserted Westminster Abbey, emptied for security reasons, on Christmas Day 1066. A disturbance outside the cathedral was wrongly interpreted as an attempt to attack the new king, and houses were torched.

William the Conqueror acquired a reputation as harsh and merciless. There were several rebellions against his rule, notably the revolt in the Fens led by Hereward the Wake in 1070, but all were successfully suppressed. As an invader and usurper, he was both feared and hated in Britain. He instigated a detailed survey of the nation's mainly agricultural resources (the so-called Domesday Book) in order to exact heavy taxes. Though uneducated, he was a gifted administrator and introduced a level of law and order to England which had not been seen for centuries.

He was riding through the burning city of Mantes during a war against Philip I of France, when his horse, startled by the flames, stumbled, throwing him forward onto the pommel of his saddle. He died a lingering death at Rouen six weeks later, at dawn on 9 September 1087, of the severe abdominal injury he sustained in the riding accident. His doctors left the moment he died; his sons had already left him; his servants stole his weapons, robes and other belongings and left the Conqueror's body half-naked on the floor.

William II

reigned 1087–1100

William II was born in about 1057, the second surviving son of William the Conqueror. According to custom, as the second son, he inherited the conquered land of England when his father died, his elder brother Robert inheriting Normandy, though the division of spoils was not agreed amicably. The year after William II's accession, many of the Norman nobles in England rebelled against the new king in favor of Robert. William appealed to the English people for help, promising them good government and a relaxation of laws, but William was like his father, hard and tough, and after the rebellion was suppressed he did not keep his promise.

His main political achievement was the conquest of the north of England and his lasting visible memorial is Westminster Hall, which was built on his orders.

William II was known as William Rufus, William "the Red," because of his red hair. William appointed the reluctant Norman bishop Anselm as his Archbishop of Canterbury, with whom he then quarreled over Anselm's determination to maintain the liberties of the Church; Anselm fled back to Normandy. William had little time for the Church, confiscating much of its property. Since in those days it was the clerics who wrote history, William's reputation has been darkly colored ever since.

An unpopular king, William was killed in a mysterious incident in the New Forest. While out hunting he was hit in the back by an arrow said to have been shot by Sir William Tyrrell, who like Anselm fled to France in fear of retribution, leaving the king's body where it fell. Whatever the truth behind the slaying of the king, no one was ever punished for it, and a conspiracy may be suspected. When William's body was eventually found, it was buried in Winchester Cathedral.

Henry I
reigned 1100–35

Henry I was born, probably at Selby, in 1068, the fourth and ablest of William the Conqueror's sons, William II's younger brother. He could read and write and speak three languages, including English. By the low standards of the time, he was well-educated. He was the only English-born son of the Conqueror, and he shrewdly decided to marry an English princess, Matilda, which was a popular decision.

When war broke out between his brothers William II and Robert of Normandy, Henry helped Robert in his defense of Normandy. In the treaty which followed (in 1091) Henry was not surprisingly cut out of the succession, but he acted with extraordinary decisiveness when William died, seizing power by seizing the royal treasure. In *de facto* control, he was accordingly elected king by the Witan. Robert nevertheless challenged him for the English throne and they fought for it at the Battle of Tinchebrai in 1106; Henry won and held his brother prisoner for the rest of his life.

In 1120 Henry took his 18-year-old son Prince William across the Channel. The ship William sailed on, the White Ship, struck a rock and sank. Prince William was drowned along with his brother and sister. Henry, sailing on another ship, fainted on hearing the news of the death of his only legitimate son and is said never to have smiled again. Touching though this story is, Henry was ruthless, uncompromising, crafty and cold-blooded; he once pushed a man off the battlements of Rouen Castle for breaking an oath of allegiance.

Without an obvious heir, Henry made the barons swear allegiance to his daughter Matilda in 1126, when she returned, widowed, from her marriage to the Emperor Henri V. Henry died at Lyons-la-Foret near Rouen on 1 December 1135, allegedly of "a surfeit of lampreys," more probably of food poisoning, and was buried in Reading Abbey.

Stephen
reigned 1135–54

❧

Stephen was born in Blois in 1097, the third son of Stephen, Count of Blois and Chartres, and Adela, the fifth daughter of William the Conqueror. His claim to the throne of England was not strong, especially since during Henry I's time he had sworn to accept Henry I's daughter Matilda as the heir to the throne. He usurped it, winning support from nobles who resented being ruled by a woman, and plunged England into a long civil war.

Stephen was good-natured and energetic but he lacked judgment and made powerful enemies, notably Matilda's illegitimate half-brother, the Earl of Gloucester. He was also unpopular because he hired lawless Flemish mercenaries. Stephen was captured at the Battle of Lincoln in April 1141, but in September exchanged for Gloucester, who had been seized by Stephen's supporters. It was then that Stephen's power increased. In 1148 Matilda left England, having reigned as queen only briefly in

1141 and she was never crowned.

In 1153 her son Henry of Anjou invaded England, Stephen's heir Eustace died, and Stephen had little choice but to recognize Henry as his heir. Stephen died of a heart attack at St Martin's Priory, Dover, on 25 October 1154, and was buried at Faversham Abbey.

The House of Anjou

Henry II
reigned 1154–89

Henry II was born at Le Mans on 5 March 1133, the eldest son of Count Geoffrey of Anjou and Matilda, daughter of Henry I of England. Against the fashion of the time, he wore his hair short. He also wore a short cloak, which gave rise to his nickname, Curtmantle.

Restless, energetic, intelligent, never content to be doing only one thing at a time, Henry was one of the ablest and most charismatic of the medieval kings. His reign was nevertheless dogged by interminable struggles to overcome the power of the great barons, the privileges of the Church and later the rebellion of his sons. He was an empire builder, inheriting England, Normandy, Maine, Touraine and Anjou, acquiring Aquitaine, Gascony, Poitou and Brittany by marriages, and conquering (or at least claiming) Scotland, Wales and Ireland. His achievement was to rule more of Europe than any other English monarch, with an empire that reached from Scotland nearly to the Mediterranean.

His greatest mistake was the intense personal conflict he allowed to develop between himself and his Archbishop of Canterbury, Thomas Becket, who was finally assassinated on Henry's orders in 1170, an act which did the king irreparable political harm. He made a further mistake in appointing his son Henry titular king in the same year. This went to the young man's head and he led a rebellion in which he was killed. Henry's approach to his three legitimate sons was "divide and rule," but it led to endless plotting.

Henry II died, beaten and intensely unhappy, of a fever in Chinon Castle on 6 July 1189, and was buried in Fontevrault Abbey.

Richard I
reigned 1189–99

Richard the Lionheart was born at Beaumont Palace in Oxford on 8 September 1157, the third son of Henry II and Eleanor of Aquitaine. He succeeded Henry II and was crowned at Westminster Abbey on 3 September 1189.

Richard was a great warrior king who spent little time in England – only six months altogether. Siding with Philip II of France, he waged war on his own father, a war in which Henry died. Together with other Christian kings, Richard launched the Third Crusade against Muslim rule in the Holy Land. He conquered Cyprus, retook Jaffa and Acre, failed to retake Jerusalem, but secured from Saladin the right for Christians to visit the holy places. Richard made enemies among his fellow Crusaders and on his way home he was captured (in spite of his disguise) in Vienna by Philip, Duke of Austria, and kept in various castles for a year and a half until a huge ransom was paid for his release – a sum amounting to three times his annual income. He returned to England briefly, but left it again (in the capable hands of the Archbishop of Canterbury) to wage a five-year war against Philip II in France.

He died at Chalus on 6 April 1199 after being shot in the shoulder by a French archer. Richard was a strange mixture of virtues and vices. Nicknamed Lionheart, he was cruel, generous, charismatic, irresponsible, brave and heedless of the plight of his people. His wars – and his ransom – drained England of its resources and weakened the monarchy.

John
reigned 1199–1216

✤

King John was born at Beaumont Palace in Oxford on 24 December 1167, Henry II's youngest son, succeeding to the throne of England and western France on his brother's death. He tried unsuccessfully to take the throne during Richard's imprisonment (which would have saved a lot of money) and was banished for a time when Richard returned. The brothers were nevertheless soon reconciled and John was named as heir. When John succeeded to the throne, he imprisoned his nephew Arthur of Brittany, a rival claimant to the throne with a stronger claim. John himself is believed to have murdered Arthur in prison. John made several other notoriously bad decisions, including rejecting the pope's candidate for the Archbishopric of Canterbury, Stephen Langton. The pope's response was spectacular; England's churches were closed and John was excommunicated (1208–9), forcing him to give in. John also antagonized his barons and precipitated a civil war.

In 1215, John was forced to sign Magna Carta, which limited royal power and outlined the powers and rights of barons and freemen. He unwisely crossed the Nene estuary at Sutton during a rising tide; when the tide came in his baggage train was lost in the Wash. The crown jewels have never been recovered. He died of dysentery on 18 October 1216, at Newark Castle while fighting a new outbreak of civil war.

The House of
Plantagenet

❦

Henry III
reigned 1216–72

❦

Henry III was born at Winchester on 1 October 1207, the eldest son of King John and Isabella of Angouleme. He was crowned at Gloucester Cathedral on 28 October 1216, and again in Westminster Abbey in May 1220. He reigned for an incredible 56 years – incredible because of his incompetence.

He succeeded to the throne at the age of nine. From 1227 he ruled extravagantly through friends and relations. Wales descended into anarchy; he lost

Poitou and Anjou; he became the only English king ever to be defeated in battle by a French one. His military adventures drove him to ask the barons for more money. They in turn forced him to accept far-reaching reforms in the Provisions of Oxford (1258), but he did not honor these and a Barons' War broke out in 1264, led by Simon de Montfort, who defeated the king in the Battle of Lewes and set up the first English Parliament. Henry's son Edward defeated and killed de Montfort at Evesham (1265), becoming effectively England's ruler.

Henry's remaining years, years of weakness and senility, were spent overseeing the rebuilding of Westminster Abbey, dying in Westminster Palace on 16 November 1272. Henry was highly cultured and ambitious, but impractical and cowardly. His appalling kingship nevertheless precipitated the creation of Parliament, regularized dealings between nobles and monarch, and strengthened the legal system.

Edward I
reigned 1272–1307

Edward I was born in Westminster Palace on 17 June 1239, the eldest surviving son of Henry III and Eleanor of Provence. Nicknamed Longshanks because he was tall, Edward was a great war-lord, strongly stamping his authority on the north, Wales (1277–83) and Scotland (1295–1300). He made his authority over Scotland forcefully felt by carrying off as a trophy the Stone of Destiny, the ancient Scottish coronation stone, and installing it in Westminster Abbey. In 1301 he created his fourth son, born at Caernarvon Castle, Prince of Wales. He defeated both John Balliol (1296) and William Wallace (1298), but died at Burgh-by-Sands near Carlisle on 7 July 1307, on his way to deal with Robert the Bruce.

Edward I was the first truly English king, and (by contrast with his father) a phenomenally able ruler. He was a soldier of genius, a masterful administrator and a great legislator. His love for his first wife,

Eleanor of Castile, was deep and genuine. When she died in 1290, he had a series of 12 beautiful stone memorial crosses built to mark the places where her body rested on its way south through England for burial; some Eleanor Crosses still survive.

Edward II
reigned 1307–27

❧

Edward II was the fourth son of Edward I and Eleanor of Castile. He was appointed first English Prince of Wales when he was born (in Wales) on 25 April 1284. Edward was an effete and completely incompetent ruler, who allowed a succession of favorites to wield power for him. The most conspicuous of these were Piers Gaveston, a flashy and conceited young Gascon knight, and Hugh le Despenser (father and son). This antagonized the barons, who forced him to banish Gaveston in 1311; they judicially murdered Gaveston in Warwick when Edward allowed him to flout the banishment in 1312. In 1314, the Scots under Robert the Bruce defeated the English army at Bannockburn and gained their independence.

This major defeat was largely due to Edward's refusal to let his army rest before the battle; Edward himself fled ingloriously from the battlefield, and did not stop until he reached Dunbar, 60 miles away. In

1326 an exiled baron, Roger Mortimer, returned from France not only with an army but with Edward's queen, Isabella, as his mistress. Mortimer and Isabella succeeded in unseating the Despensers and deposing the king. Edward was forced to abdicate on 20 January 1327 at Kenilworth. He was incarcerated at Berkeley Castle where on 21 September that year he was secretly murdered by being disemboweled with a red-hot poker.

Edward III
reigned 1327–77

Edward III was the elder son of Edward II and Isabella of France, born at Windsor Castle on 13 November 1312. He was crowned at Westminster Abbey on 29 January 1327, at the age of 14, just a week after his father's cruel murder.

He began to rule on his own account in 1330, when he killed Roger Mortimer, who had ruled on his behalf. The young Edward thus avenged his father's deposition and murder. Edward III was a majestic and affable king, who was also an outstanding military commander. He led what were at the time the greatest army and navy in all Europe in lengthy wars against Scotland and France. He failed to defeat and subdue the Scots outright, and succeeded only in launching the Hundred Years' War against France. His inroads into French territories were such that he could call himself King of France (1340) and this (exaggerated) boast was perpetuated by all subsequent English kings until 1801. He won notable victories at Sluys, Crecy (1346), Calais and Winchelsea, while his son oversaw the great victory at Poitiers (1356).

At first, Edward was immensely popular because of his good looks, good nature and agreeable manner, but the English became disillusioned when it was clear that he would sacrifice all of them in his pursuit of war for its own sake. His later reign was dominated by nobles once again struggling for supremacy and by the Black Death which killed almost a million of his subjects.

Edward III died at Sheen Palace on 21 June 1377 after reigning for 50 years.

Richard II
reigned 1377–99

Richard of Bordeaux was born in Bordeaux on 6 January 1367, the only surviving son of Edward the Black Prince and Joan of Kent. Richard was a flawed personality, on the one hand tyrannical and violent-tempered, on the other ineffectual.

His reign was dominated by major upheavals outside his control: the misrule of John of Gaunt, who governed during his minority, the expensive Hundred Years' War with France, the Peasants' Revolt sparked by the Black Death and a poll tax. The Peasants' Revolt gave the 14-year-old king his finest hour. He fearlessly rode out of London to meet an angry mob of peasants, demanding to know their grievances. Richard granted their petition for freedom on the spot and defused the situation; later, however, he reneged on his promise. He had the Duke of Gloucester and other opponents executed, murdered, imprisoned or exiled. Henry Bolingbroke was banished in 1398, and returned from exile with an army when Richard seized his estates, leading a successful coup.

Richard was imprisoned, forced to abdicate on 29 September 1399, and secretly murdered in Pontefract Castle on 14 February 1400. His main achievement was the introduction of the handkerchief.

The House of Lancaster

❖

Henry IV
reigned 1399–1413

Henry IV, Henry Bolingbroke, was born at
Bolingbroke Castle in Lincolnshire in April 1366,
the eldest son of John of Gaunt and Blanche of

Lancaster. Though descended from Edward III, he was not Richard II's rightful heir. The eight-year-old Edmund of March was descended from Edward III's third son, while Henry was descended from Edward III's fourth son. Henry was a classic usurper, the strong man on the spot with the power to take the throne, so Edmund was pushed aside.

Henry's appointment to the throne by Parliament on 30 September 1399 had the effect of giving Parliament itself much greater power than before, and Henry was wise enough to treat it with polite circumspection. He was a tactful, cautious man, good at negotiating, but in spite of his abilities he had to deal with wave after wave of rebellion and he became increasingly unpopular.

He was finally stricken with a combination of horrible medical conditions, thought to be epilepsy, syphilis and eczema or leprosy. On 3 November 1411, Henry's last Parliament met. There was dissension because Bishop Beaufort rashly proposed that the king was too ill to rule and should abdicate. The king was furious and took action against Beaufort, replacing him as Chancellor with Arundel in January 1412. On 20 March 1413, Henry IV's last fit seized him and he was carried to the Jerusalem Chamber.

While he lay unconscious, Prince Henry, his son and heir, came in and took the crown, possibly for safe-keeping, possibly to try it on. Unfortunately the king regained consciousness, noticed that the crown had gone and reproved the prince for being too impatient.

Henry IV died immediately afterwards. It had been prophesied that he would die in Jerusalem.

Henry V

reigned 1413–22

❧

Henry V was born at Monmouth in 1387, the surviving (second) son of Henry IV and Mary de Bohun. He was an able, popular and charismatic leader who turned England into the strongest state in Europe. He cut his teeth fighting Welsh rebels while Prince of Wales, and became a brave, fearless but cruel soldier. After becoming king he revived the old English claim to France and with it the Hundred Years' War. He famously won the Battle of Agincourt (1415). When news of the great victory reached London, very early in the morning of 29 October 1415, people rose from their beds to ring all the church bells in London. Henry's ship arrived at Dover on 17 November, and enthusiastic subjects rushed into the sea to carry the king ashore. Henry went on to conquer Normandy (1417–19) and reached Paris (1419), securing the Treaty of Troyes (1420) which named Henry heir to the throne of France.

Henry V died of dysentery at Vincennes Castle

near Paris on 31 August 1422, while trying to enforce these claims. He is remembered as a thoroughly admirable and heroic figure, largely because of the Shakespeare play, but he had religious dissidents burnt and achieved nothing in the way of improving the lot of ordinary English people.

Henry VI

reigned 1422–71

Henry VI was the only child of Henry V and Catherine de Valois, born at Windsor Castle on 6 December 1421, succeeding to the throne when only nine months old when his father died on campaign. Henry had the distinction of being crowned king three times: at Westminster Abbey in 1429, at St Denis in Paris two years later and again at St Paul's Cathedral in 1470. These repeated coronations did nothing to improve him as a king, and it was disastrous for him and the country that he was a pacifist at such a time.

During his childhood, power was wielded by rival ministers of the houses of York and Lancaster, notably Richard, Duke of York, and Edmund, Duke of Somerset. Humphrey, Duke of Gloucester, was President of Council during Henry's childhood, but the Council was divided into factions: Gloucester's and Bishop Beaufort's. When Beaufort became a cardinal, Gloucester tried to get him dismissed from Council because he represented the pope's interests not the king's. Beaufort became so troublesome that in 1429 it was thought safest to bring the arrangement to an end and crown the king. So it was that Henry was crowned at the age of seven, as if he was competent to govern on his own. He was nevertheless kept under the charge of the Earl of Warwick, who had been his father's companion-in-arms and who had fought under Henry IV at Shrewsbury.

After Henry VI suffered a severe (and entirely understandable) mental breakdown in 1453, fighting broke out between the houses of York and Lancaster. Henry was seized first by Yorkists and then by Lancastrians. Yorkists declared him deposed (1465) yet briefly restored him to the throne (1470–1).

Richard of York's son Edward defeated and killed Richard Neville, Earl of Warwick, then had Henry murdered in the Tower of London on 21 May 1471. Henry VI was a mild and scholarly man, absorbed in educational and spiritual matters: he was not the king needed by the times. His subjects thought him a figure of fun, as he always appeared in public in the same old blue gown; they expected a king to cut more of a dash than that.

The House of York

❧

Edward IV
reigned 1461–83

Edward IV was born in Rouen on 28 April 1442, the eldest son of Richard, Duke of York, and Cicely Neville. Edward was the first Yorkist king, defeating, deposing and murdering the Lancastrian Henry VI in the dynastic Wars of the Roses. In 1461, at the age of 18, he led an army to defeat the Lancastrians at

Mortimer's Cross, avenging the death of his father, "The Protector" Richard Duke of York. Edward captured Henry VI and became king on 4 March 1461. He created his brother George Duke of Clarence and his brother Richard (later Richard III) Duke of Gloucester; he also had an Act of Parliament passed immediately proclaiming Henry IV, Henry V and Henry VI usurpers – all of them – and himself the true hereditary sovereign.

On 1 May 1464 Edward IV secretly married Elizabeth Woodville, the daughter of Sir Richard Neville, at Grafton in Northamptonshire. It was the peculiar nature of this marriage that made it possible later for Richard III (Edward IV's younger brother) to argue that Edward V was illegitimate, thus clearing the way for Richard's own accession.

Edward IV was himself deposed by an army led by the Earl of Warwick and Henry VI's wife Queen Margaret in October 1470 and had to flee the country. He nevertheless returned the following spring to crush Warwick at the Battle of Barnet (April 1471) then Margaret at the Battle of Tewkesbury (May 1471). After Tewkesbury, Margaret's son was stabbed to death in cold blood by Richard, Duke of Gloucester (later Richard III), on his brother Edward

IV's orders, while Edward arranged the secret execution of Henry VI in the Tower. In 1478, Edward ordered the execution of his brother George, Duke of Clarence, also in the Tower.

Edward IV was a savage, ruthless king. In spite of all this mayhem, he oversaw a boom in the English economy, fostering growth in the wool trade, and was the first monarch to die financially solvent since Henry II. Edward IV died suddenly and unexpectedly at Westminster Palace on 9 April 1483, allegedly worn out by debauchery.

Edward V
acceded 1483, uncrowned

Edward V was born on 2 November 1470, the eldest
son of Edward IV and Elizabeth Woodville. As
Prince of Wales he succeeded to the throne when his
father died on 9 April 1483, but he fell victim
straight away to his uncle's ambition.

Richard, Duke of Gloucester, arrested the
Woodville family, causing such terror that Queen
Elizabeth sought safety in Westminster Abbey.
Richard placed Prince Edward and his younger
brother Prince Richard in the Tower, then in the run-
up to the planned coronation declared them illegitimate (10 June 1483). Parliament agreed to this,
fearing the instability of another long minority, and
proclaimed Richard king. The princes in the Tower

were never seen again, and are believed to have been murdered by Richard's agents in September 1483. Skeletons likely to have been theirs were discovered under some stairs in the White Tower in 1674.

Edward V was never crowned king, though he was the rightful heir, and his miserable reign lasted only 77 days.

Richard III
reigned 1483–5

Richard III was born at Fotheringhay Castle on 2 October 1452, the fourth surviving son of Richard, Duke of York, and Lady Cecily Neville. He was the last Yorkist king. He usurped the throne that rightfully belonged to his nephew, Edward V, and died in the Battle of Bosworth, the battle that ended the Wars of the Roses and launched the House of Tudor.

Richard was a great soldier who ably supported his elder brother Edward IV against Henry VI's Lancastrian backers. His reign was short and insecure. After having himself proclaimed king in preference to his nephew, Richard had to deal with a rebellion led by a disaffected supporter, the Duke of Buckingham, whom he had beheaded. He faced growing opposition from nobles who knew his claim to the throne was weak.

At the Battle of Bosworth on 22 August 1485, Richard III died, bravely fighting one of the rival claimants to the throne, the Earl of Richmond,

Henry Tudor. Richard III was far from being the repulsive villain of folklore. He was certainly cynical and ruthless, as any successful medieval king had to be, and he may have had the princes in the Tower murdered, but he was also a popular king, and an able administrator who boosted trade and introduced financial reform.

The House of Tudor

Henry VII
reigned 1485–1509

Henry Tudor was the only child of Edmund Tudor and Margaret Beaufort, great-great-granddaughter of Edward III. He was born at Pembroke Castle on 28 January 1457. By marrying Elizabeth of York he merged the two houses of York and Lancaster, ending the Wars of the Roses. His main achievement was to restore stability and peace in England.

Henry VII nevertheless had to crush rebellions and pretenders to the throne like Lambert Simnel (1487) and Perkin Warbeck (1497). Henry interviewed Perkin himself, craftily introducing him to a group of young men who had been the companions of the dead Richard, Duke of York; Perkin broke down and admitted that he knew none of them and that he was not Prince Richard. It was only with reluctance and after further trouble that Henry ordered Perkin's execution.

Henry VII was tough, crafty and hard-headed, yet also courteous. He greatly enhanced England's wealth and status by making six commercial treaties. He backed the Cabots' voyages from Bristol to the New World, encouraging an outreach to the Americas that would last for centuries. He entertained lavishly and his table is said to have cost him £14,000 a year. He was nevertheless personally frugal and miserly, and he spent his spare time going over his accounts and calculating his expenses.

Henry VIII
reigned 1509–47

Henry was the second son of Henry VII, born at Greenwich Palace on 28 June 1491. In his twenties, Henry VIII was strikingly good-looking, handsomer than Francis I of France, with whom he liked to compare himself. On hearing that Francis had grown a beard, he grew an auburn one himself. He was an accomplished musician and composer, a horseman and jouster, an excellent linguist, a devout Christian and also a huntsman and sportsman. He was very fond of tennis. A Venetian ambassador wrote: "It is the prettiest thing in the world to see him play, his fair skin glowing through a shirt of the finest texture."

In later life he became grotesquely obese and an increasingly tyrannical streak emerged, his personality possibly soured by his failure to produce a legitimate male heir to the throne. His attempt to produce an heir through a succession of disastrous marriages is legendary. He married, in succession, Catherine of Aragon (1509), Ann Boleyn (1533), Jane Seymour (1536), Anne of Cleves (1540), Catherine Howard (1540), Catherine Parr (1543). His two daughters, Elizabeth, by Ann Boleyn, and Mary, by Catherine of Aragon, both eventually succeeded to the throne. His son by Catherine of Aragon, Henry, Prince of Wales, died in infancy in 1512, and his son by Jane Seymour, Edward VI, became king on Henry's death.

Henry was a king whose sheer forcefulness is unparalleled in modern times. Henry's ruthless, tyrannical side is exemplified by his destruction of the 823 monasteries and abbeys in England, and the execution of political opponents.

Henry VIII died at St James's Palace on 28 January 1547, probably of syphilis, and was buried in St George's Chapel, Windsor.

Edward VI

reigned 1547–53

Edward VI was born at Hampton Court Palace on 12 October 1537, and he succeeded to the throne at the age of nine when his father died. During his minority England was ruled by the Lord Protector, the Duke of Somerset, until he was overthrown by the Regent, John Dudley, Duke of Northumberland, in 1550. Edward was a devout Protestant and supported Somerset's and Northumberland's attempt to consolidate the Reformation in England. Edward himself was unable to achieve much, dying of tuberculosis at the age of only 15. Under pressure, he removed his half-sisters from the succession, leaving his crown to Northumberland's daughter-in-law, Lady Jane Grey.

Edward VI died at Greenwich Palace on 6 July 1553, and was buried in Henry VII's Chapel, Westminster Abbey.

The House of Grey

Jane

reigned 1553 uncrowned

Lady Jane Grey was born in September 1537, the daughter of Henry Grey, Marquess of Dorset, and Lady Frances Brandon (daughter of Henry VIII's sister). Jane was the unfortunate victim of a plot to seize the English throne. She reluctantly married Lord Guildford Dudley as part of Northumberland's scheme to shift the succession from the Tudor to the Dudley family. It was Northumberland who badgered the dying Edward VI to leave Jane the throne. Jane was declared queen on 10 July 1553, but had no widespread support. Her reign came to an end after only nine days, when her successor had her confined. After the Wyatt Rebellion in Jane's favor, Mary I could not afford to let her live, and Queen Jane, the Nine Days Queen, was executed in the Tower on 12 February 1554. She was blindfolded on the scaffold, too far from the place where her head was to be cut off, and had to grope her way to the block, a pathetic sight which touched all who saw it.

The House of Tudor
(resumed)

Mary I
reigned 1553–8

Mary was born on 8 February 1516 at Greenwich Palace, the only surviving child of Henry VIII and Catherine of Aragon. On her half-brother Edward's death, she was faced immediately with a life and death struggle against the cause of the pretender, Lady Jane Grey. Her supporters successfully defeated Jane's and Mary was proclaimed queen on 19 July 1553.

A convinced Catholic, Mary set about reversing

Edward VI's Reformation, suppressing Protestantism in England. Her persecution of 283 Protestant martyrs, including the former archbishop, Thomas Cranmer, as well as many ordinary people, earned her the nickname Bloody Mary. She rather unwisely married King Philip II of Spain (in Winchester Cathedral), and this made her even more unpopular with her subjects. She died of influenza at St James's Palace on 17 November 1558, in the end reluctantly accepting her Protestant half-sister Princess Elizabeth as her heir.

Elizabeth I
reigned 1558–1603

Elizabeth was born on 7 September 1533 at Greenwich Palace, the only child of Henry VIII and Ann Boleyn. She cultivated, from her coronation onwards, a public image of herself as an icon of monarchy; this had to be supported and pandered to even by her closest courtiers. It was an extremely successful strategy. Elizabeth was astute, cautious and crafty, but also a forceful and willful ruler. She resisted all attempts by her advisers to marry her off, and similarly fended off all her many suitors, perhaps (consciously or unconsciously) fearing her mother's fate. Her reign coincided with an English Renaissance in the arts, trade and maritime adventuring.

Elizabeth interrupted people frequently, so she often misunderstood what they were trying to tell her. The custom developed of writing letters to the Council reporting what had been said to her, as she herself often misrepresented it. She was haughty, conceited and "majestical," quick to rebuke well-intentioned courtiers. At 60 her teeth were alternately black and yellow; many were missing, so that it was difficult to understand what she said when she spoke quickly. She eventually died at Richmond Palace, on 24 March 1603, of blood poisoning brought on by an abscess on her tonsils, after a reign lasting over 44 years.

8

❦

The Kings and Queens of Great Britain (or the United Kingdom) 1603–

The House of Stuart

❧

James I
reigned 1603–25

℥lizabeth I died childless, and her nearest living rela-
tion was James VI of Scotland, the son of Elizabeth's
much-feared cousin, Mary Queen of Scots. James had
been crowned King of Scotland at Stirling in July
1567. He was glad to become King of England
as well, and worked towards the Union of the two

countries, though he never succeeded in integrating their legal systems. The United Kingdom (of England, Wales, Scotland and Ireland) dates from his accession on 24 March 1603. He emphasized rule by divine right, though the English Parliament tried to make it clear that his powers were circumscribed by long custom. He brought his children up in his belief, and so prepared the way for the Civil War and the execution of his heir.

James I looked fat, but only because he wore baggy and loose-fitting clothes. He liked to have his breeches well padded. He was fearful by nature and had his doublets quilted against attack by stiletto. While he was in his mother's womb, her favourite, David Riccio, was torn from her side and stabbed to death, and some believe that this, together with his mother's later fate, explains his timorous nature.

It was fear of upsetting a foreign power that made him agree to the state trial and execution of Sir Walter Raleigh – for antagonizing Spain. Partly through meanness, he never changed his clothes until they were worn to rags, and only ever washed the tips of his fingers. Offsetting these unprepossessing characteristics, he was very witty, lived peaceably and died in peace, unlike many of his more charismatic predecessors.

Charles I
reigned 1625–49

Charles I was born at Dunfermline Palace on 19 November 1600, the second son of James VI of Scotland (I of England) and Queen Anne.

Charles took over from his father the idea that kings were divinely appointed to rule, and his stubborn refusal to compromise was his downfall. A small, refined, civilized and artistic man, Charles I had a very regal manner and expected always to be treated with respect and reverence. In return he was always elaborately courteous. Even in an argument he would say, "By your favor, sir, I think otherwise," and give his reasons. He was very chatty, especially with artists, engineers or travelers, from whom he could learn something. He wanted to learn, yet strangely had very few books.

Charles I was a great horseman, a good husband and father, but not the best of rulers. His first major clash with Parliament came when they would not grant him any more money for expensive foreign wars; his response was to dissolve Parliament. Then he attempted to arrest five dissident MPs – almost incredibly – by entering Parliament himself. The result was the Civil War (1642–51). A Parliamentarian army finally defeated the Royalists at the Battle of Naseby (1645), and Charles I was captured shortly afterwards. He still refused to compromise, believing that Parliament could not function without a king.

Charles would not back down so he was tried for treason and executed at Whitehall, on 30 January 1649. He wore two shirts that cold morning, so that he would not shiver. He did not want people to think he was afraid to die. It is said that Cromwell went to see the body, gazing at it intently, even lifting the head to check that it was really severed. The only words on the coffin were "Carolus Rex 1649."

The Commonwealth (Interregnum)

❧

Oliver Cromwell
Lord Protector 1653–8

Oliver Cromwell was born in 1599 in Huntingdon, where he inherited a small estate in 1617. He studied Law in London, then became MP for Huntingdon. In the early days, he dressed very plainly indeed, and with his fat red face cut a poor figure, though later he got himself a London tailor. As a young man he had a sharp, poorly modulated voice, but later became eloquent, especially when fired by anger.

In Parliament he came into direct conflict with Charles I, and during the Civil War he created the formidable regiment of "Ironsides," pressed for a no-compromise outcome to the war and took command of the New Model Army. He pressed for Charles I to be tried for treason and was among those who signed his death warrant.

Cromwell naturally filled the gap left by the king's death (1649) and in December 1653, after Charles II had been seen off, Cromwell was created Lord Protector. This made him effectively king. In 1657, Parliament offered him the crown. He hesitated, refused, but kept the right to appoint his successor – a disastrous choice, as it turned out. As time passed, Cromwell acquired more dignity, developing a regal bearing. To an extent, Charles I had been right: Parliament needed a king. It was Charles they didn't need.

Oliver Cromwell – or King Oliver as he was widely known – died in 1658 and was buried in Westminster Abbey with the crown he had declined resting on his coffin. At the Restoration in 1660 his body was dug up by Royalists, hung on a gallows at Tyburn and beheaded. This was their revenge for the execution of Charles I, who was now seen as a saint and martyr.

Richard Cromwell
Lord Protector 1658–9

❧

Richard Cromwell was born in 1626, the third son of Oliver Cromwell. He succeeded his father in September 1658 only because his two elder brothers were already dead. He was nevertheless his father's nominee, and he became Lord Protector. The job was quite simply beyond his abilities, and after a few unsatisfactory months he abdicated (May 1659). He was nicknamed Tumbledown Dick because of his failure to maintain the Commonwealth.

At the Restoration (1660) he wisely went to France to miss the purge. He returned to England in 1680 and lived very quietly at Cheshunt under the assumed name John Clarke (just in case anyone felt like settling a score) until his death in 1712.

The House of Stuart
(resumed)

Charles II
reigned 1660–85

Charles II was born on 29 May 1630 at St James's Palace, the eldest surviving son of Charles I and Henrietta Maria. After his father's execution, Charles technically acceded to the throne of Great Britain and Ireland, and briefly became king of Scotland; he was proclaimed King of Scots in 1651. Then he and a Royalist army were decisively defeated at the Battle of Worcester (1651) and he only escaped from the country with great difficulty and after many adventures. On one occasion he had to hide in an oak tree to escape capture. Eventually he reached the south coast and sailed safely across to France. He spent the next nine years in impoverished exile in France and the Netherlands.

Charles II was recalled by Parliament at the Restoration of the monarchy in 1660.

He had no sense of religion, apparently. He said he thought that God would not make him miserable for taking a little pleasure. This was a clever ploy, concealing his covert Catholicism to avoid trouble with Parliament. As he said, he did not want to go on his travels again. He was not an intellectual, but nevertheless he was interested in a great many things. He was an everlasting talker, but tended to tell the same stories again and again. He did not enjoy work, though he conscientiously did what was necessary.

He enjoyed a well-deserved reputation as a rapacious womanizer. The pretty and witty comedy actress Nell Gwyn was perhaps the best-known of his many mistresses. She is said to have urged Charles to found the Chelsea Hospital, and had at least one illegitimate son by him, Charles Beauclerk, Duke of St Albans. He had no legitimate offspring, but 14 illegitimate children among whom his favorite was James, Duke of Monmouth, and young Monmouth was later to lead an ill-fated rebellion that would result in his own beheading when Charles II died.

Charles II died at Whitehall Palace on 6 February 1685, revealing at the last moment to his assembled court that he had been a Catholic all along by sending for a Catholic priest. The secret had been well kept.

James II
reigned 1685–8

James II was born at St James's Palace on 14 October 1633, the second son of Charles I and Henrietta Maria. James shared his father's belief in the divine authority of kings. While his brother was alive, James dissembled his religion; but once he was king he was openly Catholic. These two things together meant that a collision with Parliament was inevitable. He was a womanizer like his brother Charles II, but his taste in women was unwise, even by Charles II's standards. Charles joked that his brother's mistresses were visited upon him as punishments for earlier sins.

James had considerable reserves of courage, but he lost his nerve (he suffered badly from nosebleeds when agitated) when Parliament invited William to invade.

He fled down the Thames estuary, but was stopped

at Sheppey, where the boat missed the tide. The sailors who detained him were uncertain who he was, but described him (fairly accurately) as "a hatchet-faced old Jesuit" and "a cunning old rogue." They searched him for clues to his identity and found two diamond-encrusted buckles. James coolly explained that they were only glass. Meanwhile, in London it was realized he had gone, and mobs gleefully ransacked Catholic churches, building bonfires of their books and furniture.

James II was taken (complete with black wig) to an inn at Faversham, where in the midst of a mob he boldly ordered bacon and eggs for breakfast, just to show what an ordinary fellow he was. But he was soon recognized and sent back to London, where he feared he would be executed.

In fact James II's return complicated William of Orange's position. From William's point of view, James's ignominious flight meant an empty throne and an easier passage onto it. There was a short delay, and James II's second attempt to escape to France was successful, and his abdication was announced on 12 February 1689.

James II died in exile of a stroke at St Germain-en-Laye on 6 September 1701.

William III
reigned 1685–1702

and

Mary II
reigned 1685–94

William of Orange was born in The Hague on 4 November 1650. He was Stadtholder of the Netherlands (since 1672) when he and his wife were invited by James II's Protestant opponents in England to come over and take the throne from him. William sailed with a Dutch invasion fleet, landing at Torbay. Later he met opposition from the Irish and Scots.

William was an able and conscientious politician who understood how coalitions worked. He was nevertheless aloof and distant, which made him very unpopular with his new British subjects. He died at

Kensington Palace after a fall from his horse on 8 March 1702.

William's wife Mary was the real heir to the throne, as eldest surviving daughter of James II. Parliament found that the throne could not be offered to her alone, as there was no possibility of William coming to England as a mere consort; so the throne had to be offered to them jointly – unique in British history. Mary II was good-natured, selfless and extremely popular, with the English just as she had been with the Dutch. She died at Kensington Palace of smallpox on 28 December 1694, leaving no children to succeed her.

Anne
reigned 1704–14

Queen Anne was born at St James's Palace on 6 February 1665, the second daughter of James II. She was the sister of the late Queen Mary II.

Anne was religious, dull and domesticated. She enjoyed the company of women friends, especially Sarah Churchill, wife of the first Duke of Marlborough. Her lack of interest in the broader issues and her lack of charisma made her a disappointing candidate for monarchy. She was married to Prince George of Denmark, and she gave birth to 17 children, including stillbirths; in spite of these sterling efforts, none of her offspring survived her, so once again the succession was a problem.

Anne died of a stroke at Kensington Palace on 1 August 1714. With her the Stuart dynasty ended.

The House of Hanover

George I
reigned 1714–27

George I was born on 28 May 1660 in Hanover, the eldest son of Ernest, Elector of Hanover, and Princess Sophia. Because the previous two monarchs had left no direct issue, an Act of Settlement of 1701 arranged for the British succession to pass to Princess Sophia and her Protestant heirs. Sophia was a granddaughter of James I of England, so it was through her that the Hanoverian King Georges were related to earlier British monarchs. The succession nevertheless lacked transparency, and George I had to deal with an insurrection, the First Jacobite Rebellion (1715), in favor of the Stuart claimant to the throne.

George I was a reserved, dull, awkward German who never bothered to learn English. He did not understand English politics and did not want to. When he succeeded to the English throne, he was so unenthusiastic about it that he delayed traveling to his new kingdom for seven weeks. He was thoroughly disliked in Britain, partly because he was foreign and refused to speak English, partly because of the assertive and ugly mistresses he kept, partly because he imprisoned his wife.

George I died on 11 June 1727 while visiting Osnabruck in Hanover, by chance in the same room in which he had been born. He was buried in Hanover, and is therefore one of the very few British monarchs not to have been laid to rest in Britain.

George II
reigned 1727–60

George II was born in Hanover on 30 October 1683, the only son of Crown Prince George of Hanover (later George I) and Princess Sophie. Curiously, George II at first did not believe the news of his father's death. George I had died at Osnabruck and news reached London on 14 June, the messenger carrying it straight to Sir Robert Walpole's house at Chelsea. Though it was late evening, Sir Robert drove at once to Richmond Palace, where the Prince and Princess of Wales were staying. When Sir Robert arrived, the prince was already in bed with Caroline, and a lady of the bedchamber was sent in to fetch him. He emerged, angry, flustered, half-dressed and holding his breeches in his hand to hear Walpole's news. He watched, astonished, as Walpole lowered his vast bulk to a kneeling position to tell him of his father's death and his own accession. George's response was, "Dat is one big lie." Can he possibly have believed this was Walpole's idea of a joke?

George II was nevertheless a courageous soldier and was the last British king – the last in a very long line – to lead his army into battle: it was the Battle of Dettingen (1743). The Hanoverian dynasty suffered another onslaught in the shape of a Second Jacobite Rebellion (1745–6), in favor of Prince Charles Edward Stuart, Bonnie Prince Charlie. This rebellion almost succeeded in toppling George II; only the reluctance of English Catholics to join the Stuart army caused it to turn back at Derby. George's son William Duke of Cumberland, pursued the rebels northwards relentlessly and destroyed them with unusual brutality.

George II was prepared to be guided by his ministers, such as William Pitt the Elder and Robert Walpole, and this development was a significant step towards the model of constitutional monarchy for the nineteenth and twentieth centuries. George II was a stubborn, fussy little man obsessed with detail, but also shrewd and straightforward. He was often guided by his formidable wife, Queen Caroline.

George II died of a heart attack at Westminster Palace on 25 October 1760.

George III
reigned 1760–1820

𝕲eorge III was born at Norfolk House, St James's Square, London, on 4 June 1738, the son of Frederick, Prince of Wales, and Princess Augusta of Saxe-Coburg-Gotha. His very long reign of 59 years saw the country's population double, its imports and exports quadruple, the economy industrialized, and Britain emerge as the principal power in Europe.

George himself was a conscientious father and family man, a fervent patriot and (initially) a very popular king. With 15 children, he was the most prolific royal begetter of legitimate offspring since Edward III. He was, perhaps more significantly, one of the most likeable kings Britain has had.

Unfortunately, what most people remember about

George III is that he was mad. He had his first attack of porphyria, a rare, hereditary, progressive and incurable condition, in 1765. Eventually he had to be confined at Windsor Castle, while his unreliable son George became Prince Regent (5 February 1811). Deaf, blind, unhappy and hopelessly isolated by his insanity, George died at Windsor on 29 January 1820. The cause of death is uncertain.

George IV

reigned 1820–30

❧

George IV was born at St James's Palace on 12 August 1762, the eldest son of George III. He had already ruled as Regent for nine years when he came to the throne, where he remained for a further ten years. He secretly married Maria Fitzherbert, a Catholic, in 1785 and this embarrassing mistake had to be annulled so that he could marry a wife acceptable to the establishment. He agreed to marry Caroline of Brunswick on condition that Parliament paid off his debts.

George IV was clever with a certain amount of wit. But he was an extravagant spendthrift and notoriously dissolute. He was responsible for the bad-taste absurdities of the Royal Pavilion, a kind of early seaside fun-palace at Brighton. His undisciplined behavior made not only the king but the institution of the monarchy unpopular in Britain. The king was corpulent. His former friend, the dandy George Brummell, said, loudly enough for the king to hear,

"Who's your fat friend?" This did nothing to slow Brummell's slide from favor.

George IV died, probably of cirrhosis, at Windsor Castle on 26 June 1830.

William IV

reigned 1830–7

❦

William IV was born at Buckingham Palace on 21 August 1765, the third son of George III and Queen Charlotte. He was 64 years old by the time he inherited the throne from his brother George IV. He was a simple, warm-hearted old sailor, very genial, breezy and quite eccentric. Nicknamed the Sailor King and Silly Billy, he was held in far greater affection than George IV. William had served in the Royal Navy during the American War of Independence.

As a young man he was a womanizer, like his brother; even in maturer years he was not a very serious man, but he did take his duties as king more seriously than his brother. He favored moderate social reforms, though not enough to meet the radical demands of many of his subjects.

William IV had two daughters by his wife, Queen Adelaide, both of whom died in infancy, and ten children by his mistress, the actress Dorothea Child.

William IV died at Windsor Castle on 20 June 1837, of pneumonia and liver failure.

Victoria

reigned 1837–1901

Queen Victoria was born at Kensington Palace on 24 May 1819, the daughter of the Duke of Kent (fourth son of George III) and Victoria of Saxe-Coburg. She was William IV's niece. Succeeding to the throne at the age of 18 on 20 June 1837, she had much to learn about statecraft and she was lucky to have Lord Melbourne at her side as her first Prime Minister. She had not been educated in a way suitable to her new role. Her ideas about royal powers came from her uncle, King Leopold of the Belgians, who assumed his niece would act as her own Prime Minister. Lord Melbourne successfully averted this dangerous foreign influence and assumed the position of the queen's private secretary. He tactfully and painstakingly educated her, and did so without in any way misusing the situation for personal or party political ends.

She was also lucky in her choice of husband. Prince Albert of Saxe-Coburg-Gotha, whom Victoria married in 1840 and made Prince Consort in 1857, took a keen interest in politics, science and the arts and was very active in influencing the course of events both through his wife and on his own account. It was Albert who was largely responsible for the hugely successful Great Exhibition, a huge trade fair promoting British goods and achievements. One of the main social events of her early reign was the Eglinton Tournament (1839), a week-long party at which members of high society wore medieval costume; during this, Victoria was preoccupied with devising a way of proposing to Albert – both difficult and embarrassing, because she was by nature shy and timid.

Victoria loved Albert deeply, and was grief-stricken at his unexpected early death in 1861. She retired from public life, living in seclusion at Balmoral in Scotland and Osborne on the Isle of Wight. She received the nation's sympathy initially, but her subjects grew increasingly dissatisfied with her invisibility as the years passed and she had to be persuaded to make some public appearances as the restlessness increased. While shut away from the world, without stirring she became empress of a quarter of the land area of the world and a quarter of the world's people. The first country in the world to industrialize, the United Kingdom had become the world's richest nation. Victoria herself cannot be credited with any of this; she was simply the monarch at the time when it happened.

Victoria was a homely, family-oriented woman who set the high moral standards that are often disparagingly called "Victorian," and re-established a more dignified image for the monarchy. During her reign, much of the monarchy's remaining power was surrendered, leaving Parliament as a collective ruler; it was in effect a fulfillment of the Parliamentarian cause in the Civil War.

Queen Victoria died after a short illness at Osborne House on the Isle of Wight on 22 January 1901. Her reign of 63 years and 216 days made her Britain's longest-reigning monarch.

The House of
Saxe-Coburg-Gotha

❧

Edward VII
reigned 1901–10

Edward VII was born at Buckingham Palace on 9 November 1841, the eldest son of Queen Victoria. Because of his mother's longevity, Edward waited a long time to become king. He spent this time shooting, sailing, horse-racing, gambling and philandering. He succeeded to the throne at the age of 59, and did much to bring the monarchy back into the limelight, where many people wanted to see it. An affable, sociable man, Edward was very popular, gaining the affectionate nickname Tum-tum.

His wife Alexandra knew about his widely publicized affairs but remained publicly silent and loyal to him, bearing him six children. Occasionally the mask slipped. Edward and Alexandra had a massive row about his behavior in the carriage bearing them to their coronation. It continued as they got out at Westminster Abbey, still shouting at each other. Edward roared, "Eef you shall not be qviet, you shell not be crownt!" He never lost the German accent he picked up from his German tutor.

Edward VII died of bronchitis at Buckingham Palace on 6 May 1910.

George V

reigned 1910–36

George V was born at Marlborough House in London on 3 June 1865, the second son of Edward VII and Alexandra. He had five children by his wife, the formidable Princess Mary of Teck: David (Edward VIII), Albert (George V), Mary, Henry, George Edward and John.

George was not an intellectual or even a clever man – his favorite pursuits were shooting and stamp-collecting – but he knew his limitations and performed his duties carefully and conscientiously and won wide respect. He started his career in the Royal Navy early (1877) and rose, no doubt assisted by his royal status, to the rank of vice-admiral. He was created Duke of York in 1892. As Prince of

Wales he had represented his father on visits to various parts of the British Empire. During the First World War he regularly visited the Western Front. As a direct result of this war, he changed the name of the royal family from Saxe-Coburg-Gotha to Windsor, in an attempt to dissociate the family from its German origins.

George V was a habitual smoker from an early age and contracted lung cancer. He made a partial recovery, convalesced at Aldwick near Bognor, but had a relapse. Early in the New Year, 1936, he managed to go for rides on his white pony, Jock, but on 17 January he wrote in his diary for the last time, "A little snow and wind. Dawson arrived. I saw him and feel rotten." He sat by a fire in his bedroom at Sandringham wearing a Tibetan dressing gown, dying on 20 January 1936. In his bathroom was found the Rillaton Cup, a priceless bronze age gold beaker that had gone missing many decades earlier. The king had been using it as a toothmug.

The House of Windsor

❧

Edward VIII

acceded 1936, uncrowned

Edward VIII was born at White Lodge, Richmond Park, on 23 June 1894, the eldest son of George V and Queen Mary. His love affair with Mrs Wallis Simpson (1896–1986) was his undoing. On succeeding to the throne he decided to marry Mrs Simpson and wanted her to be queen. The British establishment would not countenance the crowning of an American divorcee; Edward married Mrs Simpson on 3 June in France and was consequently forced to abdicate on 10 December 1936 after a reign of 325 days.

It seems the establishment was secretly relieved to have this excuse for getting rid of him; evidence was mounting that Edward VIII was going to be a weak, flashy, indiscreet and politically unreliable king who would damage both the country and the monarchy. Later events, such as the ex-king's indiscreet wartime meetings with fascists, bore this out.

His long retirement as the Duke of Windsor brought him little happiness. There was no role for him, no return to England, and no reconciliation with the royal family. His touching grand gesture of throwing away the throne for "the woman I love" remained the most memorable thing he did. While he lay dying of cancer, the present queen, Elizabeth II, took pity on him and paid him a visit, a gesture which he greatly appreciated. He died in Paris on 28 May 1972.

George VI

reigned 1936–52

✣

George VI was born (as Prince Albert) at York Cottage, Sandringham, on 14 December 1895, the second son of George V. He was a shy, modest, slightly built man who was not really prepared for kingship. As the king's second son, he had no reason to suppose he would ever have to endure the high public exposure of kingship, and he was mortified by his brother's abdication: he did not want to be king. He was nevertheless powered, like his father, by a strong sense of duty, and he won universal respect for his exemplary conduct during both war and peace.

During the Second World War he and Queen Elizabeth chose to continue living in London, sharing in the privations of the Blitz and risking the bombs. He had a bad stammer, and worked hard to overcome it, never shunning public speaking commitments. His great courage in these matters inspired admiration.

His very happy family life owed much to a wise

choice of wife. He married (1923) the charming Lady Elizabeth Bowes-Lyon (now Queen Elizabeth the Queen Mother), by whom he had two daughters, the princesses Elizabeth (born 1926) and Margaret (born 1930). His queen proved to be immensely popular, one of the best-loved queens in British history.

In 1949, he became Head of the British Commonwealth of Nations following the dissolution of the British Empire. After the Second World War, the days of king-emperors seemed to be over. In 1951, he opened the Festival of Britain.

George VI was a habitual smoker like his father and contracted lung cancer. He was terminally ill when he waved goodbye to his daughter Elizabeth on the airport tarmac as she boarded a plane for an African tour. The tense, drawn expression on his face showed that he knew he would never see her again. He died at Sandringham House on 6 February 1952.

Elizabeth II
reigned 1952–

❧

Elizabeth II was born at 17 Bruton Street, London W1, on 21 April 1926, the elder daughter of the Duke and Duchess of York (later George VI and Queen Elizabeth). She succeeded to the throne, as she has said, too soon. She began her reign feeling untrained, unready, and had to learn how to do the job as she went.

Elizabeth was educated privately and trained in military motor transport with the Auxiliary Territorial Service in the Second World War. She married Lieutenant Philip Mountbatten, the impecunious only son of Prince Andrew of Greece and Princess Alice (great-granddaughter of Queen Victoria), on 20 November 1947. This love-match produced four offspring: Charles, Prince of Wales (born 14 November 1948), Anne, Princess Royal (born 1950), Andrew, Duke of York (born 1960) and Edward (born 1964).

Elizabeth has continued her father's and grand-father's tradition of unremitting, unstinting loyal service, and her conscientious commitment to an arduous program of inspections, official opening ceremonies, tours and state visits has inspired wide respect. She has been a dutiful queen at a difficult time, when the role and even the need for the monarchy has been increasingly called into question. A wrong turning seems to have been taken when subjects were invited first by Christmas broadcasts, then by a television documentary, to see the royal family as some sort of model of family values. The marital problems, first of Princess Margaret, then of Prince Charles and Prince Andrew, invited more public interest – and criticism – than was welcome to the royal family. These developments have caused Elizabeth herself evident personal disquiet and unhappiness. The divorce of Prince Charles and Princess Diana and the subsequent tragic death of Diana in Paris (1997) caused many to wonder how realistic it is to expect a family to function normally under such intense media scrutiny.

Elizabeth II's personal interests are rural; she likes country walks and dogs and enjoys owning and running racehorses. Behind a rather dour, cautious and stoic public face, she also has a mischievous sense of humor. She is a good mimic.